THE
LONG
ARC
OF
LEADERSHIP

Copyright © 2025 James E.H. Mayer

All rights reserved.

No part of this publication may be reproduced, stored in a retrieval system, or transmitted in any form or by any means—electronically, mechanical, photocopying, recording, or otherwise—without the prior written permission of the publisher, except by a reviewer who may quote brief passages in a review.

First Edition
Published by Praxis Legacy Press
California, USA

Paperback ISBN: 979-8-9994395-0-5
Hardback ISBN: 979-8-9994395-1-2
Ebook ISBN: 979-8-9994395-2-9

Book design and interior layout by Alan Hebel

Library of Congress Control Number: 2025914219

Printed in the United States of America

For more information or to request permission to quote or reproduce material from this book, please contact:
TheLongArcBook@gmail.com

THE LONG ARC OF LEADERSHIP

Leadership Lessons

From a Life of Global Service

JAMES E.H. MAYER

PRAXIS LEGACY PRESS
California, USA

TABLE OF CONTENTS

Dedication vii
Preface xi

The Long Arc of Leadership 1

Part I: Presence 9

1. Walk Slowly 11
   A Korea Voice 31
   Leadership Takeaways 32
   Transition from Walk Slowly to Listen Deeply 33

2. Listen Deeply 35
   A Korea Voice 51
   Leadership Takeaways 52
   Transition from Listen Deeply to Lead Lightly 53

3. Lead Lightly 55
   A Korea Voice 62
   Leadership Takeaways 64
   Transition from Lead Lightly to Trust Wisely 65

4. Trust Wisely 67
   A Korea Voice 95
   Leadership Takeaways 97
   Transition from Trust Wisely to Hope Fiercely 98

Part II: Belief 99

5. Hope Fiercely 101
    A Korea Voice 113
    Leadership Takeaways 115
    Transition from Hope Fiercely to Love, Always 117

6. Love, Always 119
    A Korea Voice 135
    Leadership Takeaways 137

Part III: Legacy 139

7. Lead So Others Remember 141

8. Some Final Thoughts 145

Acknowledgments 149

Part IV: Final Tools 151
    Reflections for Future Leaders 153
    Quick Guide for Leaders 157
    The Long Arc of Leadership Framework 159
    Leadership Practice Guide 161

Bibliography 175
Index 179
About the Author 183

DEDICATION
In Gratitude to the Korea Foundation

This book is offered in deep gratitude to the president and staff of the Korea Foundation (KF), whose vision, generosity, and kindness rekindled the spirit of Peace Corps Korea and stirred memories that had never truly faded.

In 2008, the Korea Foundation opened a door many of us thought long closed. Through the Peace Corps Korea Revisit Program, they called us home—those of us who had once come to Korea as Peace Corps volunteers and American staff, wide-eyed and hopeful, carrying little more than a dream of making a difference.

What they gave us was something we didn't even know we had longed for: the chance to return. To walk again on the soil that shaped us. To see a Korea transformed—modern, resilient, radiant—and yet still remembering.

And so we came. More than 400 of us, so far. Some arrived with spouses, children, and grandchildren—now grown. All came with full hearts and hesitant anticipation.

We found a Korea reborn. Cities where fields once lay. Light and innovation where once we lit candles against the dark. We met former students, now teachers. Former patients, now doctors. Former colleagues, now silver-haired friends.

And to our astonishment—we had not been forgotten. Korea remembered.

We returned to the schools, the clinics, the alleyways where we had once labored and laughed and learned. And we, too, remembered:

The sting of winter air. The buzz of summer cicadas. The weight of chalk dust on our fingers. The folded note from a student. The scent of garlic, the sound of a bow, the comfort of being called in for tea.

We remembered who we had been—and who we had become—because Korea had once opened its heart to us.

And most of all, we remembered that while we came to serve, we stayed to learn. From Korea, we learned resilience, reverence, and the quiet power of community. Lessons that shaped the lives we led long after we returned home.

In offering us this full circle of return, the Korea Foundation gave us more than a program. They gave us healing. Reflection. Perspective. They helped us see, with gentler eyes, what our small efforts had meant—and how deeply Korea's generosity had reached.

Years later, during the quiet uncertainty of the COVID-19 pandemic, the Korea Foundation reached out again. Across oceans and sealed borders, they sent "Survival Boxes." But what arrived was something more: Not just sanitizer and snacks, but kindness. Dabang coffee, a photo, a note. Love, folded carefully between each item.

And with each one, we felt again:

The warmth of friendship.

The comfort of being seen.

That service, once shared, binds hearts beyond time.

Dedication

In those uncertain days, those boxes glowed like lanterns. They reminded us who we were—and who we still are. Friends of Korea. Forever.

To the Korea Foundation, and to the people of Korea, I offer our deepest thanks.

Thank you for remembering us. Thank you for welcoming us back.

Thank you for showing us that the bonds forged in humility and hope do not fade. They deepen.

Because of you, Peace Corps Korea is not a closed chapter.

It is a living story—echoing still in classrooms, clinics, and in every heart that once served and still cares.

With love, remembrance, and friendship always,

Jim

PREFACE

Leadership is rarely loud. It can be as quiet as sitting on the floor of a rural schoolhouse in the Korean countryside and listening to a young volunteer wrestle with homesickness or self-doubt. Leadership is also trusting a local counterpart who sees a possibility you had never considered...or choosing to walk beside rather than ahead.

As country director for Peace Corps Korea, I had the rare privilege of witnessing leadership emerging in classrooms and medical clinics, in small government offices and around kitchen tables, where a mixture of language sometimes faltered but connection rarely did.

This book was born from these moments.

What I learned in Korea reshaped my understanding of leadership, not as a means of control or authority, but as way to build relationships. I realized that, at its core, true leadership was rooted in six enduring truths:

Walk Slowly.
Listen Deeply.
Lead Lightly.
Trust Wisely
Hope Fiercely
Love, Always.

These weren't lessons from policy papers. They came from experience, hard earned, often tender, and always humbling. They emerged not from my role as a director, but from my role as a student of the people and the culture around me. Let me illuminate these truths.

Walk Slowly

In Korea, I learned the power of patience. I learned that relationships cannot be rushed, and that moving slowly does not indicate a lack of ambition, but is a sign of respect. I came to understand that every meaningful connection, every sustainable change, began not with momentum, but with presence. Walking slowly allows you to see what you would have missed—the nuance, the texture, the humanity beneath the surface.

Listen Deeply

Leading Peace Corps volunteers required a kind of listening that extended beyond words. It meant listening for what was unsaid, for what lived in the silences between cross-cultural misunderstandings or the weight behind a volunteer's quiet *I'm fine*. It meant listening to our Korean hosts, to their hopes, their history, and their wisdom. Deep listening was a way of honoring others, of building trust not through answers, but through attention.

Lead Lightly

As country director, I carried responsibility, but I quickly learned that leading lightly was often more powerful than leading hard. Volunteers didn't need me to dictate; they needed me to believe in them, guide them gently, and then step aside when they found their stride. Our Korean partners didn't need another foreign expert. Instead, they needed a collaborator, someone who understood that influence is most enduring when it's shared.

Trust Wisely

Trust, in a cross-cultural context, is sacred. It must be given with care and received with humility. I learned to trust volunteers to establish their own learning curves, and to trust Korean communities, respectful of their own solutions. I came to understand that trust is finding the courage to invest in others and the discipline to do so with wisdom.

Hope Fiercely

I arrived in Korea on the cusp of a remarkable transformation. The country was no longer recovering from war but rising into a position of global leadership. Nevertheless, the echoes of its past remained in every story shared, every memory honored. I watched volunteers place their hope in small gestures, one student, one class, one patient, one disabled child, one relationship at a time. I saw Koreans place their hope in us, in the idea that strangers could become family. That fierce hope, so resilient, sometimes fragile, always brave—fueled us all.

Love, Always

In the end, leadership is about love. Love for the work. Love for the people we serve. Love for the future we may never fully see, but choose to believe in. As country director, my love for Korea and its people deepened every day. Not through grand events, but through events as ordinary as a shared meal, a quiet walk. A handwritten note left on my desk. This love, steady, simple, and sustaining, became the truest compass of my leadership. The people around me felt my love, and returned it in kind.

This book reflects these values…my values. It is not a textbook, nor is it a memoir in the traditional sense. It is a written meditation on what it means to lead with humanity, to serve with humility, and to believe, always, in the power of people to transform one another.

To the Korean teachers, partners, and officials who welcomed the Peace Corps with grace, and to the volunteers who served with courage and open hearts: thank you. You shaped me far more than I ever shaped you.

To those stepping into leadership today, in any corner of the world, I offer these reflections not only as a road map, but as a hand extended.

Remember, you do not have to lead perfectly. But if you walk slowly, listen deeply, lead lightly, trust wisely, hope fiercely, and love, always, the arc of your leadership will stretch farther than you can imagine.

In gratitude of your service,

Jim

THE LONG ARC
OF LEADERSHIP

It was the end of November 1978 when I first set foot on Korean soil. The moment the airplane door opened onto Gimpo Airport, a blast of cold, dry air rushed in, a knife cutting through my jacket. That air smelled of jet fuel, sharp and metallic, carrying an undercurrent of burning leaves from somewhere beyond the tarmac. Loudspeaker announcements barked in rapid-fire Korean, echoes bouncing off the cavernous gray walls of the arrivals hall. Uniformed porters darted past me, pushing carts stacked precariously high with battered luggage and crated goods. It was chaos.

I tightened my grip on my suitcases and stepped into a mass of humanity. Businessmen in dark suits and carrying briefcases hurried, elderly women bundled in heavy coats leaned for support on what I guessed were grandchildren. And soldiers, the ever-present soldiers, stood watch with rifles near the exit doors, their breathing sending steam into the frigid air.

I was thirty-six years old and the newly appointed Peace Corps country director for Korea. In those suitcases, stuffed between briefing books and spare ties, were all my ambitions, and a significant quantity of doubts.

I stepped out of the terminal. There was Seoul, this vast sprawl rising beneath a pale, brittle sky. The jagged mountains encircling the city loomed, their peaks dusted with the season's first snow. They felt ancient to me, solemn, and somehow watchful.

I pulled my coat tighter and took a deep breath. Like the smell inside the terminal, I could taste the pungent blend of diesel exhaust, roasting chestnuts from street vendors, and the icy bite of approaching winter.

I was prepared for Korea. Or so I thought. I'd spent long nights poring over histories of the country, accounts of Japanese colonial rule, of brutal wars fought and refought on its soil, of a people who refused to be broken. I thought I knew resilience.

I thought I understood perseverance. But no book, no briefing, prepared me for what awaited.

Behind my official papers and practiced words, I carried a private, gnawing weight that I shared with no one. I had never been a Peace Corps volunteer. Unlike most of my colleagues, I had not spent years living in mud-walled villages, learning languages through laughter and survival, sharing rice bowls with strangers who became family. I came not as someone who had *walked the walk*, but as someone tasked with leading others. I had no romantic illusions about Peace Corps service, nor did I embrace the kumbaya sentiment that was sometimes projected onto it. This was the Peace Corps, and its mission was too important to be diminished by popular—but largely misleading—notions that it existed solely to broaden Americans' horizons rather than to leave something of enduring value behind.

It was my firm belief that the Peace Corps wasn't a job; it was a mission. It was based on the concept that people working with people, shoulder to shoulder, sharing knowledge, sharing hardships, sharing dreams—together, we could build something better than what had come before. And here, in Korea, this mission was urgent.

As much as Korea tried to move away from it history, the scars of the past were still fresh. Memories of a horrifying colonial occupation; the devastation of the Korean War, with families torn apart and cities reduced to rubble, these were the images that still shaped the landscape. Across the heavily fortified DMZ, the threat of violence continued. Poverty was not just visible; it was visceral. I could feel it in the drafty schoolrooms where students huddled in their coats around a single stove for warmth, and in the dirt alleys where children played among construction debris and rusted bicycles.

And yet, what would soon strike me more deeply than the hardships was a kind of current pulsing beneath it all. It felt like a fierce, almost electric, determination to thrive.

Peace Corps volunteers were scattered throughout the country, from bustling cities to remote mountain villages. They worked alongside Korean doctors and nurses, battling tuberculosis and leprosy, along with other diseases that ravaged communities. The volunteers served as maternal and child-health workers, so needed in those rural clinics where sharing even basic information about handwashing and nutrition was saving lives.

There were community services performed by the volunteers. They helped launch the country's first Special Olympics, working with Civitan International, and created education awareness programs to bring into the light children who had long been hidden due to misplaced family shame. These selfless individuals trained Korean English-language teachers to better equip them for the classroom, and they taught English not as a skill, but as a key that opened doors to universities, careers, and conversations with a world far beyond the Han River.

I was eager to lead these men and women, eager to support this noble work. But I learned quickly that professional titles and good intentions meant little in Korea.

My biggest challenge wasn't the language—though my clumsy Korean sparked warm chuckles more often than not. Nor was it the cultural differences, which were real and many. Instead, I soon learned that my greatest challenge would be establishing trust.

Trust from our Korean staff—dedicated professionals who had weathered too many foreign advisors breezing in with grand plans…only to leave before those plans could take root. I would come to understand what Jon Keeton, one of the earlier country directors of Peace Corps Korea, once said:

"The Korean staff took their responsibilities very seriously. I often called them our heart, soul, and conscience—and they deserve much of the credit for what volunteers achieved."

And trust, too, from the volunteers—many of whom had endured hardships I could barely imagine: isolation, illness, homesickness, and the slow, grinding difficulty of change that never comes fast enough. And yet they remained—determined to use their skills and share them with others.

My first months as the Peace Corps director in Korea were humbling. There were so many obstacles and challenges that I hadn't anticipated.

As my leadership role moved forward, I began to understand that I was too quick to speak, too slow to listen. I misread silences, missing those nuances that hid in the spaces between words. My well-meaning ideas sometimes landed like heavy stones in a pool of water, causing disruptive ripples and, in too many cases, unintended and unfortunate consequences. You might say that I was on a learning curve that thrust me into a realization that I had much to learn.

Many nights, after lengthy meetings accompanied with polite smiles, unspoken misgivings, and doubts, I wandered Seoul's seemingly endless labyrinth of alleys. I passed food stalls where *ajummas*, middle-aged women, wrapped in thick scarves, flipped sizzling pancakes over hot griddles, their cries of *"Hotteok! Hotteok!"* piercing the night. I wove through students huddled together under bus stop awnings, textbooks pressed to their chests, their breath resembling threads of silver clouds in the darkening sky. I walked past grimy storefronts with neon lights buzzing above windows, the smell of boiling broth and burnt sugar clinging to the cold.

And as I walked, I asked myself if I was failing.

I recall catching my reflection in a shop window. My eyes seemed tired, my shoulders hunched against the cold. The sting of self-doubt coursed through me. Was I cut out for this? Or was I just one more outsider making promises he couldn't keep?

Then came the night that changed everything.

Mrs. Lee, a senior member of the Korean staff, a woman whose quiet grace masked a life of extraordinary endurance, invited me to dinner. She chose a back-alley restaurant tucked behind a row of blinking shop signs and narrow stairwells. The kind of place I never would have found on my own.

Inside, the place was warm, almost stifling, the air thick with garlic, soy sauce, and woodsmoke. I struggled to sit cross-legged on the thin cushions that circled the low table, the area warmed from below by an ondol heating system, using direct heat transfer from wood smoke to warm the underside of the floor. I soon learned that this was the traditional Korean way of heating an area.

Dish after dish arrived. There was thinly sliced *bulgogi*, marinated slices of beef, sizzling in a cast iron pan, bowls of *doenjang jjigae* bubbling with earthy soybean paste, and plates of kimchi so sharply fermented it almost stung my nose.

As we ate, I fumbled with my chopsticks and she laughed softly. She showed me how to wrap a perfect *ssam*, a bite of meat and rice tucked into a crisp lettuce leaf with a dab of fiery red pepper paste.

As we ate, she began to tell her story. And as she spoke, her voice was calm, almost detached, but her words cut with the precision of a scalpel. She was six years old when the war came, and one evening at dinnertime, there was a pounding on the door. A policeman warned her family that North Korean troops were only miles away and they needed to escape. The family grabbed what little they could and fled their home, with Mrs. Lee clutching the schoolbooks she had received that same day and the sound of artillery thudding closer and closer.

She told me how they walked mile after endless mile for more than six weeks, making their way through a country being torn open by violence. How they hid under bridges while planes dropped bombs and strafed the area, like fire raining down from above. She recalled seeing friends and neighbors fall behind, some never to be seen again. She spoke quietly of the three surgeries she endured to repair a herniated muscle in her thigh—without anesthesia, the doctors' hands trembling, her parents holding her down, praying the entire time. As we continued our meal, she shared the hope for the future of her children, wanting desperately for them to live in a Korea free from war, free from hunger. A country on a course that would take them to a better life for its people.

Her story wasn't dramatic; it was raw, unvarnished. She wasn't seeking pity or praise from me. She was simply telling me the truth of her life.

As I listened, really listened, I began to realize how little suffering, how few challenges, I had experienced in my life. Every description she shared reminded me how easy the path had been for me.

With a new understanding, I could see that brick by brick, life by life, Korea was building a future with a fierce determination that no foreign aid package or diplomatic speech could manufacture. They didn't need directors or dignitaries handing down solutions; they needed allies and partners. They needed witnesses to chronicle the truth.

That night, something shifted inside me. Perhaps the most important awareness was that leadership wasn't about commanding from a position of superiority, but walking alongside, listening with an open heart and a closed mouth. Leadership was about patience. Humility. And it relied on creating a true sense of solidarity.

The next day, and in the weeks and months that followed, I could feel myself changing.

For one thing, I stopped trying to fix things quickly. I started showing up not with pronouncements but with questions. I sat with the Korean staff in their cramped offices as we drank endless cups of barley tea while I asked them to teach me what they knew. I rode with them along battered roads to rural clinics and schools. I visited volunteers who were scattered across the country, not to evaluate them, but to understand the realities they faced every day.

I sat on cold floors with volunteers and teachers, watching them draft lesson plans by candlelight. I stood in muddy fields with health workers who were weighing infants on makeshift scales. I shared meals, sometimes lavish, sometimes humble, with families who welcomed me as if I were a long-lost cousin.

It was because of my willingness to learn…and observe… that trust began to weave itself into my relationships.

In the dusty corridors of provincial hospitals, in drafty schools where students practiced English by shouting across freezing classrooms, in back-alley food stalls and rice paddies and tiny one-room health posts, I began to learn how leadership truly worked.

It wasn't glamorous. It wasn't quick.

It was the slow weaving of trust, thread by thread.

And slowly, change began to bloom.

I remember one winter morning arriving at a village health post where a volunteer and a Korean nurse were conducting a health workshop for mothers. The clinic had no heating, and our breath clouded in front of us as we huddled around a rickety table. The two of them demonstrated how to swaddle a newborn using an old sheet. The mothers watched, hesitantly at first, and then giggling as they tried, their faces lighting up with pride when they mastered the technique. A simple act, yet one that would save countless newborns from the lethal cold of winter.

There was the classroom where another volunteer, frustrated by the inflexibility of textbook drills, produced a worn soccer ball. She introduced a game: students had to toss the ball and say an English word or ask a question in English before passing it on.

At first, the children didn't understand. She tossed the ball to a boy seated near the center of the classroom. He froze, then threw it back. She caught it, smiled, and said "boy" as she tossed it again. Still, he hesitated.

Then another student raised his hand and asked for the ball. He caught it and shouted, "sister!"—then passed it across the room to another boy, who grinned and said, "father!"

And just like that, the class understood.

The room erupted in laughter—and suddenly, in English.

Not perfect English. But joyful, living English.

I
PRESENCE

Chapter 1

WALK SLOWLY

In a world that often glorifies rapid decision—making and swift execution, genuine leadership frequently demands a very different quality: the ability to walk slowly. This is not about physical pace. Instead, it's about a mindset. To *walk slowly* is to lead with deliberation, empathy, and presence. It means resisting the urge to fix, diagnose, or command before fully understanding. It is the choice to move thoughtfully through complex environments, to observe keenly, to listen deeply, and to act only after understanding the landscape—culturally, emotionally, socially.

Few case studies embody this leadership approach better than the Peace Corps experience in South Korea between 1966 and 1981. Over 2,000 volunteers served during this time, assigned across a rapidly developing country still healing from war and grappling with modernization. Whether in rural villages, growing industrial towns, or marginalized communities, volunteers discovered that rushing in with preconceived solutions often led to disappointment. The deepest impacts were made by those who *walked slowly*, those who immersed themselves, learned the language, built relationships, and earned trust over time.

Immersion: *Walking Slow into Korean Communities*

Peace Corps Korea was uniquely expansive. Volunteers worked across a variety of sectors: teaching English, promoting maternal and child health, assisting the disabled, serving in communities affected by leprosy and tuberculosis, and supporting other vital local initiatives. Each context demanded more than technical skills; it required cultural humility, emotional intelligence, and patience.

New volunteers arrived at their service sites with only a few months of intensive training and minimal understanding of Korea's deep cultural norms. They were briefed not just on language and technical tasks, but on what it meant to be fully present in a host community. The training staff, many of them former volunteers themselves, stressed one key philosophy: *Walk Slowly.*

Kathleen Stephens, who taught English in Yesan and later became US ambassador to South Korea, described this process of immersion vividly: "Everything I thought I knew about teaching and leadership had to be rebuilt from the ground up. Only by living side by side with my colleagues and students could I begin to understand their world and what they needed from me."

Volunteers lived with host families, ate Korean meals, used public baths, and walked the same dirt paths as their neighbors. This physical and emotional proximity helped build the foundation of trust that would shape their service. *Walking Slowly* wasn't an affectation, it was a strategy for long-term, human-centered leadership.

Leprosy Villages: *Presence Before Programs*

Perhaps nowhere was the Peace Corps Korea philosophy of "presence before programs" more essential than in the country's leprosy villages. These communities, often tucked away on the periphery of towns or hidden in rural hillsides, were home to individuals and their families who had endured not only physical suffering but decades of systemic rejection. The disease itself, medically treatable by the time Peace Corps entered Korea in the late 1960s, remained deeply stigmatized. To the average Korean, the very word *nakkyeoja* (leper) evoked fear, superstition, and isolation.

Peace Corps volunteers assigned to these villages quickly discovered that success could not be measured by the number of workshops delivered or clinics established. Their work was neither fast nor linear. It unfolded slowly, sometimes imperceptibly, through a thousand small, daily interactions that, over time, began to restore trust and dignity to the people they served.

Sarah Bartlett, a health volunteer stationed near a leprosy settlement in Jeollanam-do, described her early frustrations: "For weeks, no one would speak to me beyond curt nods. It wasn't until I spent an afternoon simply sitting with an elderly patient under a persimmon tree, saying nothing, just being present, that things began to shift. Leadership, I learned, sometimes meant shutting up and showing up."

David Kim, another volunteer working in Gyeongsangbuk-do, recalled a similar turning point: "I had planned to teach basic wound care, but no one came to the sessions. It wasn't until I started helping the village handyman carry water and fix broken steps that people began to trust me. One day, an older woman handed me a small cup of barley tea and said, 'Now you are one of us.' That moment meant more than any lesson I could have taught."

Their stories were not unique. In village after village, volunteers learned to let go of the notion that they were there to "fix" something. Instead, they became students of humility, patience, and cultural listening.

Jeannie McAllister, placed in a small compound outside Daegu, remembered her struggle to earn the confidence of the community's nurse: "She wouldn't look me in the eye for the first month. I think she assumed I was another foreign do-gooder who would take notes, snap a few photos, and leave. But I kept showing up, sweeping the clinic, sorting bandages, helping with meals. Eventually, she invited me to join her for early morning rounds. That's when things changed."

Over time, Jeannie and the nurse began co-designing basic hygiene workshops and introducing new dressing techniques. But it wasn't the programs that mattered most—it was the fact that they had become collaborators, equals in a place where hierarchy and shame had long defined social interaction.

The quiet discipline of walking slowly came to define some of Peace Corps Korea's most lasting contributions. Unlike urban assignments where volunteers faced the possibility of being swept up in institutional partnerships or rapid development projects, those in leprosy villages learned the power of presence as a form of resistance against stigma, against invisibility, and against hopelessness.

Daily life in these settlements was often quiet and monotonous. Many residents were elderly or disabled, while others bore visible scars and deformities that made traveling even to the nearest market a source of shame or harassment. Volunteers stepped into this reality not as saviors, but as neighbors. They played janggi (Korean chess) with grandfathers, helped repair cracked windows, taught English informally to curious teenagers, and occasionally mediated disputes between residents and local authorities.

But the most important gift they offered was *time*.

Peter Hwang, a second-year volunteer in a settlement near Mokpo, recounted a moment that stayed with him decades later: "One man, Mr. Lee, had lost most of his fingers. He'd never married and had no family left. Every Sunday, we'd share a pot of instant ramen and listen to old trot songs on the radio. He never said much. But after six months, he said, 'Thank you for not being afraid of me.' I think that was the first time in years he let someone see him as a person, not a patient."

The emotional toll on volunteers was often considerable. Many grappled with feelings of helplessness. The scale of suffering often felt disproportionate to what they could offer. And yet, Peace Corps Korea's leadership was intentional in supporting these assignments—not with pressure for outcomes, but with space for reflection and community. Volunteers in leprosy villages regularly corresponded with each other and regional staff, sharing strategies for building trust, processing grief, and celebrating small wins.

One of the later country directors of Peace Corps Korea reflected: "The volunteers working in leprosy villages redefined service. It wasn't about delivering medicine or health education programs. It was about being a bridge: a human face of compassion in places that had known only fear."

Over time, even the most skeptical villagers began to soften. Invitations to family dinners, offers to learn traditional games or cooking, and shy introductions to grandchildren were subtle signs of healing. Our volunteers didn't cure leprosy, but they helped cure something just as deep: the psychic wound of exclusion.

In many cases, these relationships endured long after the official service ended. Some former volunteers returned years later to visit. Others stayed in touch through letters, photos, and eventually, emails. Several continued careers in public health, social work, or medicine, crediting their time in Korea's leprosy villages as formative.

Walk Slowly, here, meant breaking down stigma, not with slogans or seminars, but through weeks, even months, of quiet gestures that proved one thing: *You are not forgotten. You matter.*

In the end, the leprosy villages of Korea taught the Peace Corps something as well. They became a kind of mirror revealing that effective development work begins not with action plans but with the courage to see others fully and to be seen in return. They affirmed that sometimes, the most revolutionary thing a volunteer can do is to simply stay.

Teaching English: *Slow down*

One of the most visible and wide-reaching assignments of Peace Corps Korea was in English education. In the decades following the Korean War, the Republic of Korea was transforming at a rapid pace, economically, politically, and culturally. As the country pushed to modernize and globalize, English became a critical skill, opening doors to higher education, international trade, diplomacy, and professional advancement. Peace Corps volunteers, many of them recent college graduates themselves, were placed in middle and high schools, teacher training institutes, and provincial education offices, as well as universities across the peninsula.

Often, these volunteers were the first native English speakers their students, and in many cases, their Korean co-teachers and principals, had ever met. Their presence alone carried the immense symbolic weight of a living link to the world beyond Korea's shores.

Even in this relatively structured and goal-driven context, success depended less on technical expertise and more on human connection. Volunteers quickly discovered that traditional Western teaching methods, interactive learning, open discussion, even casual rapport, often clashed with Korea's classroom culture, which was deeply influenced by Confucian values of hierarchy, respect, and order.

John Christopher, who taught in a rural middle school in Gyeongsangbuk-do, shared: "My Western teaching techniques fell flat. The students were shy, deferential, and terrified of making mistakes. It wasn't until I started spending time outside of class helping students with chores, attending festivals, visiting their homes, that I began to understand their world. Only then could I shape my lessons to fit their lives."

Many volunteers entered service with ambitious plans. They had curricula packed with role-playing activities, conversation drills, and games. But what they encountered were students who rarely spoke up, looked to the teacher for the "correct" answer, and hesitated to participate in anything that could single them out. The fear of losing face, of embarrassing oneself in front of peers, was stronger than any desire to experiment with a foreign language.

So, volunteers adapted. *Walking Slowly* in these classrooms meant listening, really listening, not just to what students said, but to what they didn't say. It meant noticing who avoided eye contact, who lingered after class, who copied answers word for word rather than risk being wrong.

Some Peace Corps teachers began introducing English outside the formal curriculum. In these informal settings, they launched after-school English clubs where pressure was lower and laughter was encouraged. They wrote and staged plays with students, using simple language and familiar scenarios. Other teachers taught English through Korean folk songs translated into English, or invented vocabulary games using household objects.

These innovations weren't just pedagogical tricks; they were cultural translations. The most effective volunteers realized that their job wasn't just to teach English, but to do so in a way that honored students' identities, values, and fears.

Marcia Lee, assigned to a boys' high school in Jeollabuk-do, recalled: "My students wouldn't say a word during lessons. But when I started drawing cartoon strips on the chalkboard, little sketches with speech bubbles, they began laughing and asking questions. One day a student stayed after class to show me his own drawings, with English captions. That's how we began our weekly comic club. It started with one student and ended with twenty."

Teaching English became a vehicle not just for language acquisition but to build confidence. In a rigid educational system focused on rote memorization and college entrance exams, the presence of a Peace Corps teacher sometimes created the only space where creativity, curiosity, and humor were allowed to flourish.

But these breakthroughs didn't happen in isolation. Korean co-teachers were critical partners in the process, and navigating these professional relationships required tact and humility. Volunteers had to learn how to work within a hierarchical school system where younger staff rarely challenged authority, and where deference to age and title often determined the flow of communication.

At times, the relationship between Peace Corp teachers and their Korean counterparts was one of mutual learning. Peace Corps teachers introduced new classroom ideas, while Korean teachers helped them understand school culture, student backgrounds, and parent expectations. When these partnerships worked well, they served as models for collaboration and intercultural respect.

Anna Vasquez, who co-taught in a girls' middle school in Gangwon-do, explained: "My co-teacher, Mrs. Park, had been teaching English grammar for twenty years. At first, she was skeptical of my methods. But I never pushed. I invited her to co-lead games and shared my materials. Over time, we started designing lessons together. She taught me how to command a classroom. I showed her how to make it fun. We ended up as close friends."

In some schools, volunteers were treated like a novelty, given little responsibility beyond reading dialogues aloud or running the occasional conversation class. In others, they were given full autonomy, expected to manage entire classes without training or support. In either case, volunteers had to calibrate their expectations and develop their own sense of what success looked like. Not based on immediate results, but on relationships nurtured over time.

One country director recalled that the most effective volunteers were not necessarily the ones with the strongest academic background, but those who "led with their ears." They listened to students, to colleagues, to principals and parents. In doing so, they fostered mutual respect and co-created solutions.

This act of listening extended beyond the classroom. Many volunteers lived on or near school grounds, in teacher dormitories or small rooms provided by the local education office. They ate school lunches with students, swept snowy paths in winter, attended graduation ceremonies and teacher outings. Their lives were deeply embedded in the rhythm of the school and the community.

Michael O'Donnell, who lived on the school campus in a fishing village outside Busan, wrote: "Some of the best lessons happened on the soccer field or walking home from school. I'd ask, 'What's that plant called?' and they'd teach me in Korean. Then we'd find the English word together. Language went both ways. So did respect."

Over time, many volunteers saw their roles shift from language instructor to community leader. They helped write grant proposals for school resources, supported students applying to international exchange programs, organized cultural festivals, and hosted English camps during breaks. Some worked with parents' associations to explain the children's progress or with local officials to support education initiatives.

The impact went far beyond vocabulary lists or grammar drills. Former students, years later, would recount how their Peace Corps teacher changed their perception of foreigners, boosted their confidence, or inspired them to study abroad. For many Koreans, especially in rural areas, a Peace Corps teacher was their first encounter with someone who looked, spoke, and lived differently, yet cared deeply for and about them.

In some cases, students and volunteers stayed in touch long after the assignment ended. Letters, postcards, and eventually emails flew back and forth. A handful of former students visited their teachers in the US, while others hosted them when they returned to Korea years later.

Peace Corps Korea's legacy in English education cannot be measured in test scores or textbook revisions. Its true value lay in the relationships it fostered, the trust built slowly, the laughter shared—hesitant at first, and then freely. It lay in the volunteers who learned to lead not by speaking, but by listening. And in doing so, they gave their students more than language skills... they gave them courage.

In classrooms where fear of failure ran deep, the volunteers showed that learning could be playful—and mistakes, part of the process. In schools driven by ranking and exams, they showed the value of questions over answers. And in communities wary of outsiders, they became friends.

The leadership skill of *Walking Slowly* here meant remembering that language learning isn't just cognitive, it's emotional, cultural, and deeply human. The Peace Corps teachers of Korea succeeded not because they were native English speakers, but because they stayed long enough to listen, long enough to understand, and long enough to be understood.

Maternal and Child Health: Honoring Local Wisdom

Korea in the 1960s and 1970s stood at the crossroads of a rapid transformation. While cities became modernized and industries began to flourish, rural communities often remained tethered to practices shaped by generations of tradition, scarcity, and resilience. Among the most urgent public health challenges were high rates of infant and maternal mortality, limited prenatal care, and a lack of basic sanitation infrastructure. Many rural mothers gave birth at home, often with the help of elderly midwives or traditional birth attendants known as *sanhujori halmeoni*, (literally, postpartum grandmothers). These women relied on knowledge passed down through the generations orally and not taught in institutions.

Into this complex setting came Peace Corps volunteers, many of whom had little or no formal medical training. Assigned to Maternal and Child Health (MCH) programs, they were expected to contribute to reducing infant deaths, improving maternal nutrition, and promoting healthy practices. On paper, their task was clear. In practice, it was anything but.

This work demanded a kind of leadership that could not be

taught in manuals. It required listening. Not by teaching, but by honoring the wisdom that was already there.

Margaret Ladd, an MCH volunteer in Gangwon-do, remembered: "At first, I thought I was supposed to teach the midwives how to do things better. But they didn't want lectures. They wanted to know if I respected them. Once I showed that I did, they began asking me about vitamins, clean birthing kits, and how to treat infections."

Respect wasn't a technique; it was a way of being. Volunteers quickly learned that relationships came before outcomes. Many were welcomed cautiously at first—after all, why should a young foreigner, barely fluent in Korean, be trusted with something as sacred and high stakes as childbirth?

Rather than impose change, the most effective volunteers chose to observe. They walked miles to attend village births, sitting quietly in corners of homes lit by oil lamps. They assisted with postnatal care, carried water, and held babies so mothers could rest. Slowly, trust emerged—not through authority, but through presence.

Once relationships were formed, questions flowed in both directions. Korean health workers began sharing stories of complicated deliveries, herbal remedies, and rituals meant to protect both mother and child, while volunteers offered insights from their own backgrounds. They introduced concepts such as boiling water to sterilize medical tools, having prenatal checkups to monitor fetal growth, and dietary advice that include teaching how simple protein-rich foods like eggs and soybeans provided nourishment and strength to expectant mothers.

New ideas were not introduced as corrections but as suggestions, offered with humility. And when they were accepted, it wasn't because they came from the West; it was because they came from someone who had become a trusted neighbor.

Julia Connelly, assigned to Jeollanam-do, recalled: "There was one midwife, Mrs. Choi, who had delivered more than 300 babies. I never pretended to know more than she did. But she was curious, always asking questions. So we started keeping a notebook together. She wrote down things she wanted to remember, like how to mix oral rehydration solutions or recognize signs of infection. That notebook became her most prized possession."

Volunteers often served as bridges between informal practices and the emerging national health system. At a time when Korea's Ministry of Health was expanding rural clinics and promoting modern medicine, Peace Corps workers were helping connect local communities to government nurses and public health officers. But these connections only succeeded when built on mutual respect.

Some volunteers assisted in mobile clinics, providing vaccinations and conducting health education sessions for mothers and children. Others organized workshops for coworkers, not as lectures, but as shared learning spaces where traditional knowledge met basic public health. These sessions include many facets of health practices: demonstrations on handwashing, clean delivery kits, infant nutrition. Whatever was taught was always anchored in the understanding that change takes time and must be rooted in trust.

The role of the volunteer was not to replace local wisdom but to supplement it. One Peace Corps nurse described it as *walking beside, not ahead.* That included accompanying a coworker to a night birth in freezing weather...not because she was needed, but because her presence mattered. It meant celebrating healthy births... not as personal victories, but as community achievements.

Over time, small shifts became visible. More women began to seek prenatal care. Birth attendants learned to boil water before deliveries. Mothers fed their children boiled eggs instead of only rice gruel. These weren't sweeping reforms, but life-saving changes grounded in respect, not authority.

The country director at the time reflected on what made maternal and child health volunteers so effective: "The best volunteers weren't those who thought they were smarter than the locals. They were the ones who listened, adapted, and made themselves part of the community. Walking Slowly saved lives, literally."

This work was emotionally demanding. Volunteers faced the realities of rural poverty up close: births gone wrong, children lost to infection or malnutrition, mothers weakened by hard labor and inadequate care. There were no easy solutions, no quick wins. Progress was measured in months, sometimes years.

But in the slow pace of development, something deeper was happening. Volunteers became part of the village fabric. They were invited to naming ceremonies and first-birthday celebrations. They helped carry wood in winter and rice during harvest season. In return, they were taught songs, proverbs, and remedies.

And they were loved—not for what they knew, but for how they stayed: with humility, with patience, and long enough for trust to take root.

For many former MCH volunteers, these experiences became the foundation of lifelong careers in medicine, nursing, midwifery, and global health. More than a few returned to Korea years later, some as medical professionals, others as old friends retracing the paths of their early service.

The legacy of Peace Corps work in maternal and child health wasn't built on statistics alone. It was built on memory. The memory of a volunteer sitting beside a worried mother, of a birth attended in silence and gratitude. And an American and Korean midwife laughing together over shared tea after a safe delivery.

Walking Slowly in MCH meant honoring traditions, not erasing them. It meant learning that leadership carried towels, fetched clean water, or offered a steady hand during labor. It meant recognizing that the women delivering the babies of Korea's future already had wisdom. What they needed was not instruction, but respect.

Peace Corps Korea didn't bring only new knowledge; it affirmed old truths. And in doing so, it helped improve not only maternal and child health outcomes but also the sense of dignity, agency, and connection in the villages it touched.

Working with Disabled Children: Slow Miracles

Peace Corps Korea placed some volunteers in institutions for children with physical and intellectual disabilities. In 1960s and 1970s Korea, these places were not only under-resourced, but often socially invisible. At a time when disability carried heavy stigma, the children were frequently hidden away, their futures viewed with pity at best, indifference at worst. Volunteers stepping into these spaces confronted not only logistical challenges, overcrowding, lack of trained staff, and inadequate equipment, but also deeply embedded cultural attitudes.

Here, *Walking Slowly* took on new meaning. There were no quick results, no tidy programmatic wins. Yet over time, the steady and compassionate presence of a volunteer could transform not just an institution, but the very way these children saw themselves.

Timothy O'Neill, who worked at a center in Seoul, wrote: "There were days I felt helpless. I couldn't fix a lifetime of institutional neglect. But I could show up. I could be there every day. I could notice a child's first word or celebrate when one learned to button a shirt. Leadership wasn't about big victories; it was about witnessing small miracles."

Volunteers were not trained specialists. Most had no background in physical therapy, special education, or occupational health. But they had something just as important: consistency and compassion. They went to the same room every morning. They greeted children by name. They learned which child responded to music, which one loved picture books, which one smiled only when handed a spoon with their favorite porridge.

Many volunteers assisted overworked Korean coworkers by helping with physical therapy routines, encouraging motor skills development, or simply feeding and bathing children who couldn't care for themselves. These tasks were not glamorous, but they were vital. In some cases, a volunteer's daily involvement freed up local caregivers to focus on medical needs or attend to new arrivals. In others, volunteers simply filled a gap, offering play, attention, or comfort where none had existed before.

Katherine Meyers, assigned to a facility in Daejeon, recalled: "There was a boy with cerebral palsy who had spent most of his days alone in a crib. He couldn't speak. He barely made eye contact. I started sitting next to him for 15 minutes each day, talking, singing, and reading. Months later, he reached for my hand. It was the first time he'd reached for anyone. That moment taught me everything I needed to know about what progress really means."

Sometimes, the simplest act like sitting on the floor, making eye contact, or holding a child's hand became radical gestures. In doing so, volunteers modeled to staff, families, and surrounding communities that these children were not broken, not burdens, they were human beings, worthy of time, affection, and dignity.

Volunteers also found that change often moved in unexpected directions. Some began organizing playtime outdoors, giving children their first experiences in nature. Others introduced visual aids, tactile toys, or music as tools to engage children with limited verbal communication skills. Still others taught rudimentary sign language or gesture systems to help children express basic needs.

In nearly every case, these innovations were born not of training, but of attentiveness. One volunteer noticed that a blind child calmed instantly when hearing a particular lullaby. Another realized that a child labeled as "unresponsive" began to engage when a drumbeat echoed through the room. Each breakthrough, however small, was a reminder that these children were listening, feeling, reaching out in their own ways.

A common thread in volunteer reflections was the tension between expectation and reality. Many arrived with a desire to make a difference. They left having learned that *difference* often looks like routine care done with love. As one volunteer put it: "The biggest change I made was brushing someone's hair each morning and letting them know they were seen."

Over time, institutional staff took notice. Some began to adopt volunteers' methods, incorporating play into therapy, creating visual routines, or building stronger personal connections with the children. Others saw the impact of simply slowing down and focusing on individual needs rather than institutional schedules.

One center director in Busan reflected: "When the children saw a foreigner kneel beside them and smile, they began to see themselves differently. The staff did too. We realized we had been managing them, not loving them. The volunteers helped us see a different way."

This wasn't just anecdotal. A few institutions that hosted volunteers eventually adopted more inclusive policies and began outreach to local families, or partnered with emerging Korean NGOs focused on disability rights. While volunteers didn't always drive these changes directly, their presence often served as a catalyst.

That presence was particularly meaningful to children with no visitors. In an era when families often felt shame or fear about having a disabled child, many of these young people were effectively abandoned. For them, a volunteer might be the only adult who smiled at them daily, remembered their birthday, or asked them how they felt.

Anne Crosby, who worked in Jeju, shared: "There was a girl who never spoke. Not once. But every morning, when I walked into the room and said, 'Good morning, Mi-sook,' she would clap her hands. I don't know if she understood the words. But she knew I was there. That mattered."

Some volunteers remained in touch with these children long after their service ended. A few sponsored education or therapy expenses from afar. Others returned years later, amazed to find a child they once fed now walking, speaking, or helping younger residents. These slow miracles, unfolding over time, became the most enduring legacy.

Peace Corps Korea's work with disabled children didn't just support care institutions. It began to shift perceptions of what these children could do, what they deserved, and how a society ought to value its most vulnerable members. It wasn't done through campaigns or conferences, but through day-after-day engagement. Through eye-level conversations. Through the celebration of even the smallest steps.

Walk Slowly. In these spaces, this meant sitting still long enough to hear the quiet signals of trust. It meant giving a child who had been ignored the one thing they needed most: the consistent message, spoken and unspoken, that they mattered.

In the words of a former country director: "Volunteers didn't arrive with grand strategies. They brought something better. They showed up, every day, and gave love to children no one else had time for. That's not charity, that's leadership."

A Legacy Built Slowly

When the Peace Corps program in Korea closed in 1981, some feared that its legacy would be fleeting. But the opposite proved true. The relationships built through patient, humble service endured across years, across oceans.

Many volunteers stayed connected to Korea, working in government, diplomacy, or education. They helped establish sister-city programs, scholarship funds, or NGOs. Gerry Krzic, a former volunteer and president of Friends of Korea, remained deeply involved with Korean education, wrote: *We left Korea, but Korea never left us.*

This legacy was not the result of high-profile projects or quick wins. It came from slow, consistent, human-centered leadership. From living with host families. From listening more than speaking. From leading by *Walking Slowly.*

Walk Slowly as a Timeless Leadership Lesson

Leadership today is often defined by speed. We value agility, disruption, and rapid innovation. But the Peace Corps Korea experience offers an important counterpoint: complex, human-centered work, education, health, and community development. The impact does not come from rushing in. It comes from humility, patience, empathy, and presence.

To *Walk Slowly* is not to avoid action. It is to prepare for meaningful action. It is to:
- Immerse oneself in the lives and values of others.
- Build trust not with declarations, but through daily acts of solidarity.

- Adapt approaches to fit local realities, not preconceived plans.
- Lead with compassion, humility, and deep listening.

The leader who will *Walk Slowly* sees farther, connects deeper, and builds foundations that endure long after they're gone.

"You went in and you sank or swam," said Kevin O'Donnell, the first country director of Peace Corps Korea. "My biggest job was to point them in the right direction and then get the hell out of the way."

As the world confronts enormous challenges, global health crises, educational inequities, and cultural polarization, the leadership example set by Peace Corps Korea remains as relevant as ever.

For exercises, self-assessments, and action prompts related to "Walk Slowly," see the **Leadership Practice Guide** *in the back of this book.*

A Korean Voice

Ms. Park
*Former Provincial Education Officer,
Gyeongsangbuk-do (1970s)*

When foreign programs came to our province, many came with big plans and short timelines. But we have a saying in Korea: 천천히 가면 멀리 간다—'If you go slowly, you go far.'

The Peace Corps volunteers were different. They didn't rush into our classrooms telling us what to do. They came to staff meetings, listened, asked questions, even when their Korean was poor. One volunteer visited my office every Friday for three months before we started any joint teacher training. Not to persuade me, but just to understand.

At first, I thought this slowness meant uncertainty. Later, I saw it for what it was: respect.

When you move slowly in Korea, people watch your steps. They see if you show humility. They test if you will stay. That volunteer walked slowly and, because of that, he walked far with our community. Years later, he returned to visit and was welcomed like a son.

If you want deep relationships in our culture, don't rush. Sit. Share tea. Ask about someone's parents. *Walk Slowly*, and you will be invited in.

LEADERSHIP TAKEAWAYS

Walk Slowly

In fast-paced business environments, speed is often mistaken for competence. But when leading across cultures, rushing can erode trust and miss crucial nuances. Walking slowly isn't hesitation, it's moving at the pace of relationships.

- **Observe before acting.** Take time to understand the landscape, culturally, emotionally, and socially, before implementing solutions.

- **Prioritize relationships.** People do business with those they trust, not just institutions or titles.

- **Respect local pacing.** Moving too quickly can signal arrogance; adapting to local rhythms demonstrates humility, awareness and respect.

BOTTOM LINE: Lasting leadership is never rushed. Walk slowly, build trust, and arrive with relationships that endure.

Transition from Walk Slowly to Listen Deeply

As we step forward from the intentional pace of *Walk Slowly*, we enter a space of heightened awareness. Slowing down grants us presence—but *Listening Deeply* transforms that presence into connection. By attuning our hearts and minds to others, we bridge the gap between mere proximity and true empathy.

Listen Deeply invites us to lean in—not just to the words spoken, but to the pauses, the expressions, the rhythms that carry cultural meaning. It's in those quiet spaces that we find real understanding: the weight of unspoken emotion, the nuances lost in translation, the gestures that speak louder than language.

And when we listen deeply, we honor those we serve. We validate their experiences, reflect their truths, and build the kind of trust that becomes a foundation for shared purpose. Here, in this unfolding of hearts and cultures, patience becomes purpose—and presence becomes partnership.

Chapter 2

LISTEN DEEPLY

Leadership is often portrayed as bold action, charismatic vision, or decisive decision-making. Yet some of the most enduring lessons in leadership are learned not in moments of visibility, but in quiet attention…when in deep listening. This is not a form of passive hearing, but an intentional, disciplined practice of wordlessly receiving, interpreting, and valuing others' words, silences, and emotions. This form of leadership revealed itself repeatedly as I came to understand the experiences of Peace Corps volunteers in South Korea.

Most of these volunteers were in their early twenties with limited international experience. Yet through their quiet presence, patient observation, and willingness to listen, many of them forged relationships that transformed not only their communities, but also themselves. Why? Because they demonstrated a model of leadership rooted not in authority, but in humility and empathy.

This chapter explores how the practice of deep listening shaped the Peace Corps experience in South Korea and offers lessons still relevant to leadership today. Drawing on personal stories, historical context, and cultural dynamics, it highlights how attentiveness builds trust, bridges differences, and uncovers wisdom not easily accessible through instruction alone.

A Korea in Transition

When the first volunteers arrived in Korea in 1966, the country was still recovering from the Korean War. Economic development was just beginning under President Park Chung-hee's Five-Year Plans. The contrast between urban modernization and rural poverty was stark. Most of our people were stationed in remote villages, teaching English in middle and high schools, and often were the only foreigners in the area.

This was long before the internet or global media connected the world. Many of these men and women arrived with only a rudimentary understanding of the Korean language and its rich culture. Their success as teachers and neighbors depended less on what they brought and more on how well they could observe and adapt. They had to shift from a posture of authority to one of inquiry, from speaking to listening.

For many, the first few months were humbling. They encountered unfamiliar food, complex social customs, and a deeply hierarchical society shaped by Confucian values. But over time, they found that the key to adaptation wasn't mastery of content, it was attentiveness to people.

Though Seoul was transforming rapidly, most of Korea remained rural. Villagers fetched water from wells, heated homes with charcoal, and children were taught in uninsulated classrooms. For many of our American volunteers, this wasn't a foreign country; it was another world.

Despite recognizing these differences, the Peace Corps didn't send experts or technicians in those early years. Instead, it sent young Americans, mostly teachers with a college degree and a strong desire to serve. After their orientation, their role was to teach English. However, many of these volunteers would come to understand that their deeper task was to listen.

Listening Over Speaking

In the beginning, many of them arrived with a sense of purpose. Some were driven by idealism, others by Cold War solidarity, and still others by the simple desire to help. Many believed they had something important to offer, but that confidence quickly came face-to-face with reality. If they were going to bring this important element to the table, they needed to learn about their environment.

They encountered Korean administrators who spoke sparingly yet commanded deep respect, and co-teachers who offered their most candid advice—not in meetings, but over shared bowls of *kimchi jjigae* (spicy fermented cabbage stew) and cups of *makgeolli* (unfiltered rice wine). It became clear that listening wasn't just a way to gather information, it was the foundation for building respect.

Mary Beth Gorman, who served in Jeollanam-do in 1969, remembered how her early days were marked by making mistakes, mispronouncing names, misunderstanding silences, and leading with too much Western assertiveness. She wrote in a letter home: "I realized very quickly that if I was going to survive here, I had to stop explaining and start observing."

This was a common realization. Korean society was built on deference to elders, indirect communication, and the centrality of relationships. The most successful volunteers learned to read between the lines, to observe posture, timing, and what was left unsaid. Over time, by listening to their co-teachers, host families, and students, they moved from being outsiders to becoming trusted participants.

Learning the Unspoken Curriculum

In the late 1960s and 1970s, Korean classrooms were places of discipline and ambition. Students sat ten to a row, wore uniforms, and focused on rote memorization. The Peace Corps volunteers, trained in communicative teaching methods, often felt out of step. Many tried to introduce songs, games, or group activities. Sometimes these innovations were welcomed; other times they met quiet resistance.

Those volunteers who took the time to observe first, to understand why things were the way they were, soon realized that education in Korea was not just academic; it was deeply aspirational. English was more than a subject—it was a bridge to economic opportunities, a way into elite universities, and a pathway to future security. In that context, experimentation was risky and structure was sacred.

Tom Carter, who served in Gangwon-do from 1971 to 1973, chose to observe for a full semester before suggesting changes. "I sat in the back more than I stood at the front. I asked questions at lunch. I listened when teachers vented or praised students. Only after that did I propose a new way to teach vocabulary. Because I listened, they listened back."

Listening as Cultural Exchange

Outside the classroom, life continued as a quieter, deeper form of cultural exchange. Our people lived alongside their neighbors, sharing meals, walking the same roads, and participating in daily rituals. It was in these ordinary moments, in markets, on buses, beside rice paddies, that the most meaningful connections occurred.

Korea was changing quickly. New highways and factories

signaled modernization, while television brought images from afar. But in rural communities, life still revolved around seasonal rhythms and long-standing customs. For many Koreans, a Peace Corps volunteer was the first foreigner they had ever met. And for the volunteers, Korea was often their first encounter with a culture so different from their own.

Trust was not assumed. It had to be earned. Helen Cho, a teacher in Gyeongsangbuk-do, later recalled her Peace Corps colleague: "She didn't try to change us. She always asked questions first. She wanted to understand why we did things the way we did. Because she listened, we listened to her too."

This mutual exchange, born from curiosity and sustained by attentiveness, became the heartbeat of the Peace Corps experience. It wasn't about delivering solutions. It was about sharing in one another's lives.

The Power of Shared Silence

Some of the deepest lessons in listening came through silence. In Korean culture, silence is not awkward; it is rich with meaning. It can express respect, reflection, empathy, and understanding. Peace Corps members learned that not every quiet space needed to be filled with words. Sometimes, the most powerful communication came through a shared physical presence and nothing more.

Michael Lee, a volunteer in 1977, described sitting in silence beside his host father on the heated ondol floor after dinner, sipping barley tea. He wrote in his journal, "We didn't say a word, but I felt more welcome in that moment than in a hundred words of praise. He knew I was tired. I knew he was grateful. Nothing more needed to be said."

Such moments were not rare. In a country where language barriers and cultural differences ran deep, the volunteers gradually learned to listen not just with their ears but with their whole selves. Over time, they developed the ability to sense the unspoken rhythms of village life, to know when to speak, when to wait, and when to simply sit in silence.

Listening as Leadership

From these varied encounters emerged a new kind of leadership, one built on empathy rather than control. With these new skills, volunteers didn't lead by asserting authority. Instead, they led by listening and then acting in ways aligned with what they had heard. They showed curiosity. They recognized respect as a form of influence. And they learned that effectiveness came more from humility than from charisma.

For many, this lesson shaped their lives long after their service. Some went on to become teachers, diplomats, or aid workers. Others brought these insights home, applying them in community leadership or everyday relationships.

In a time of rapid change in Korea, amid economic growth, political shifts, and rural transformation, Peace Corps volunteers discovered that the most grounded way to lead was to listen first. Not for answers, but for understanding. Across these paths, one truth endured: their deepest lessons in leadership came not from leading, but from listening.

Listening as a Survival Skill

Listening deeply in Korea wasn't just a method, it was essential. For many volunteers, it was the difference between connection and alienation. They had entered a society shaped by complex hierarchies, linguistic nuance, and unspoken expectations. Their official roles may have given them a title, but they had arrived without the cultural fluency to earn trust. Listening became their first and most important form of adaptation.

Consider a volunteer assigned to a mountain village in Gangwon-do in 1974. Eager to make a difference, he began his service with boundless enthusiasm, starting clubs, organizing games, and introducing new teaching methods. But instead of admiration, he encountered confusion. His informal tone, fast speech, and relaxed dress were seen not as friendly but as disrespectful.

It wasn't until a co-teacher gently explained the misunderstanding that he paused from his usual routine. He began watching how others carried themselves, how they bowed upon entering a room, how they used honorifics, how they paced their speech. He didn't abandon his personality, but he adjusted his style. He listened before he acted. As a result, the whispers stopped and his students began to respond. Trust began to grow.

Host Families as Classrooms

For many, host families were the most intense sites of cultural learning. These homes were filled with unspoken expectations, shared meals, floor seating, early rising, seasonal diets, and intricate family hierarchies. Few of these norms were explained outright. Instead, they had to be observed, absorbed, and understood through attentiveness.

Another volunteer who served in Chungcheong Province in the late 1970s recalled a moment early in her stay when she unknowingly offended her host mother. Wanting to help, she began washing her own clothes. The next day, her host mother was cold and distant. Meals were quiet. She was confused.

Only after speaking with her language tutor and school principal did she realize the issue. By doing her own laundry, she had implied that the family's care wasn't good enough. She hadn't meant to offend, but her well-meaning independence had disrupted the household dynamic. The next morning, she quietly placed her laundry in the shared basin. Her host mother responded with a warm smile and a second helping of rice at dinner. Trust had been rebuilt, not through apology, but through listening and respectful action.

When Not to Act

Sometimes, listening means waiting. A volunteer in Daegu became frustrated when a teacher consistently arrived late to their co-taught class. His instinct was to confront the issue directly, just as he might have done in the States, but a Peace Corps staff member cautioned him. "Watch and wait," he was told. "Ask quietly first."

He followed the advice. He soon learned the teacher was caring for aging parents in the mornings, so what had seemed like disrespect was actually a personal sacrifice. A direct confrontation would have caused embarrassment and tension. Instead, he shifted the lesson schedule to allow his colleague more flexibility. With that small adjustment, the partnership thrived.

In each of these situations, listening was not passive. It required intention, courage, and restraint. It took humility to admit one's ignorance, and patience to allow understanding to emerge. But time and again, it proved to be the essential ingredient for connection.

Listening Across Cultures

Cultural dissonance was perhaps the most persistent challenge. Those volunteers raised in individualistic, egalitarian societies found themselves immersed in a collectivist, hierarchical world where age determined status, silence conveyed meaning, and relationships trumped rules.

Those who adapted did so not by discarding who they were but by recognizing that their way was not the only way.

A volunteer was stationed in a conservative agricultural town near Daejeon in 1972, where she felt isolated at first. Male teachers avoided direct conversation and older women rarely looked her in the eye. Even students kept their distance. But instead of retreating, she started observing.

She noticed that women deferred to the principal, spoke softly, and followed established routines. So, she joined them in the school kitchen, peeling garlic, rinsing rice, and listening. Over time, she was folded into the fabric of school life, not through grand gestures, but through shared labor and quiet presence.

The volunteer later wrote, "I learned that listening means letting go of what I expect a relationship to look like. These women didn't need me to speak. They needed me to be there."

Understanding Group Harmony

A volunteer was based in Busan during the industrial boom of the late 1970s. He was assigned to a technical high school filled with students from families transitioning from farming to factory work. Eager to apply his American teaching techniques, he encouraged role-playing and classroom discussions, methods meant to inspire participation.

But his students remained quiet, and he wondered why. When he finally asked his co-teacher, the response was simple: "They don't want to stand out."

In Korea's group-oriented culture, speaking out can feel like risking group harmony. The volunteer realized that his well-meaning approach had unintentionally put students in a difficult position. So, he adapted and used group activities requiring shared answers. He also encouraged anonymous written feedback. Slowly, participation improved. He had listened not only to what was being said, but what wasn't, thereby reshaping his teaching to honor both his students' needs and their culture.

Listening to Suffering

Not all lessons came from the classroom. Volunteers often lived in communities marked by war, poverty, and trauma. Listening when these experiences were being discussed required a different kind of attention, one grounded in presence and empathy rather than solutions.

A volunteer, hosted by a widowed grandmother in a rural village, described long winter evenings sitting by the fire. Her host spoke softly, telling stories in a dialect the volunteer barely understood. At first, she could only nod. But over time, she began to grasp the meaning—not of words, but of the importance of simply being present. The elderly woman didn't want advice, she wanted to be heard.

Listening, in this sense, meant standing with others—not to fix their problems, but to honor their experiences and let them be heard.

The Quiet Power of Compassion

A volunteer who represented the Peace Corps in North Gyeongsang Province in 1978 faced resistance from his co-teacher, Mr. Choi, when he introduced role-plays and group discussions. Every idea was met with *maybe later* and the volunteer felt discouraged.

Instead of pushing, he began asking Mr. Choi about his background, his students, and his concerns. In one conversation, Mr. Choi explained that the students needed structure, explaining that they were not accustomed to speaking up. His suggestion? That he and the volunteer work together to help the students build confidence, step-by-step.

That moment shifted the dynamic. The volunteer recognized that his methods, though creative, needed to align more closely with what Mr. Choi felt comfortable supporting. He scaled back his innovative approach and focused instead on pair work, gentle repetition, and group activities that didn't single students out.

Slowly, Mr. Choi began offering ideas of his own. By year's end, they were co-leading a weekly conversation club.

The volunteer later reflected that the breakthrough came when he stopped trying to change things. Listening had built trust, and trust had made change possible.

Shared Silence, Shared Pain

A volunteer was assigned to a coal-mining town in Taebaek. He struggled to connect with his students. The boys were respectful but emotionally distant. That changed when one student, Jin-ho, lost his father in a mining accident.

The volunteer brought a small bundle of fruit to the family. He bowed, sat silently on the floor, and said almost nothing. But the silence spoke volumes. After that day, other students opened up. One asked the volunteer to join a hike. Another walked with him to the post office.

The volunteer later wrote that it wasn't his energy or lesson plans that earned their trust. It was that moment with Jin-ho, when he sat with the boy in silence.

Even today, these stories reveal that in places marked by hardship, being present matters more than being clever. Listening is often the deepest expression of caring.

The Leadership of Listening Deeply

Too often, leadership is equated with assertive speech, bold decisions, or visible action. But in Korea, the volunteers discovered a different model: leadership through listening. They didn't lead with authority; they led with humility. They didn't influence by imposing; they influenced by letting what they heard shape what they did. Listening became the foundation of trust. It shaped relationships with students, teachers, and communities. It gave volunteers credibility not as experts, but as collaborators. And it gave them the insight to act thoughtfully and effectively.

For many, this lesson endured long after service. Some became educators, others diplomats or development professionals. Nearly all carried forward an understanding of leadership rooted in empathy, patience, and respect.

A volunteer was assigned to a girls' middle school in South Chungcheong Province. It had a reputation for academic rigor and strict discipline. Eager to contribute, she proposed ideas for collaborative teaching and new clubs, but her suggestions were met with silence.

She changed her approach and began arriving early for morning assembly. She also helped with mundane tasks, such as organizing supplies, grading tests, and sweeping the floor after events. As she participated, she watched, listened, and learned how the school functioned.

Months passed. One day, a senior teacher invited her to a weekend picnic. Conversations flowed. The principal, once distant, thanked her for her dedication.

"I didn't earn their trust by being brilliant. I earned it by being steady, by showing that I respected how they did things, and that I was listening."

Her leadership wasn't loud, but it was lasting. By the end of her service, she was asked to co-lead a summer camp and speak at graduation.

Listening in Policy and Partnership

The ethic of listening wasn't limited to individual volunteers—it defined how Peace Corps Korea operated. Unlike many development programs, Peace Corps placed volunteers only where they were explicitly requested. Korean ministries, schools, and local leaders identified their own needs—and Peace Corps responded.

This approach relied on dialogue, not directives. Korean staff served as cultural interpreters, bridging expectations on both sides. They conveyed volunteers' concerns with clarity and tact, while also helping those same volunteers understand the deeper context of Korean norms, values, and priorities.

In one case, a rural school in Jeollabuk-do requested a volunteer to support students who were struggling academically. Peace Corps didn't respond with a pre-written plan. Instead, staff visited the town repeatedly, met with parents and teachers, and asked questions.

Months later, when the assigned volunteer arrived, trust had already been built. He and his supervisor visited each classroom to hear students voice their expectations. When challenges arose, they were able to handle them through an ongoing conversation, not a show of control.

"It felt like I was entering a relationship, not a job," Eric said. "Because I was invited, not imposed."

This model of reciprocal listening helped Peace Corps Korea thrive. It made change collaborative, not confrontational.

Listening as Legacy

Even decades after the Peace Corps program in Korea ended, its legacy remains, carried on through memories, relationships, and values shaped by listening.

In interviews conducted during return visits, former volunteers repeatedly named *Deep Listening* as the most important skill they learned. "It taught me how to listen with my whole body," one said. "Not just to words, but to context, emotion, and history." Another reflected, "Listening was the doorway to everything: understanding, respect, friendship."

In a fast-paced, hyperconnected world, deep listening is increasingly rare and increasingly needed. Leaders today are expected to act quickly, speak boldly, and manage complexity. But without listening, those actions lose their foundation. They become untethered from the human realities they're meant to serve.

Peace Corps Korea offers a different model. It shows that listening isn't a soft skill, it's a core discipline of leadership. It ensures inclusion by creating a space for every voice. It fosters trust through mutual respect...and uncovers needs that data may miss. Equally important, listening—really listening—shapes decisions through empathy, not ego.

For leaders in diplomacy, education, development, or any field that works across cultural differences, the lesson is simple: listen, keep the pace slow, ask questions.

It was interesting to note that, at the Peace Corps Korea 50th anniversary reunion in Seoul in 2016, Koreans who had worked with or had been taught by volunteers didn't speak about flashy lessons or projects. Instead, they remembered the volunteers who "paid attention," "really listened," and "understood us." For the Koreans, that was the legacy that mattered.

Listening Transforms

To *Listen Deeply* is not to agree with everything, nor is it to abandon one's voice. It is to take others seriously enough to seek understanding. It is to suspend judgment long enough to learn. It is to recognize that wisdom is often gained and expressed in moments of quiet.

The story of Peace Corps Korea is not just one of service; it's a story of unexpected transformation. Many volunteers arrived expecting to bring change but found themselves changed instead. They came to teach, to lead—but through listening, they learned. And in that listening, they discovered that the most enduring leadership begins not with control, but with humility and mutual respect.

In an age hungry for authenticity, the call is clear: *Listen Deeply.* And not only to understand others, but to be transformed yourself…and transform the world around you.

Ready to dig deeper into "Listen Deeply"? See the **Leadership Practice Guide** *in the back of this book for tools and reflection prompts.*

A Korean Voice

Ms. Lee
Former High School English Co-Teacher, Gyeonggi-do
(1970s)

At first, I was nervous to work with the American. I worried he might take over the class or correct me in front of the students. But he didn't do that. On the first day, he asked how I wanted to divide the lesson. I said we could each take half. But instead of rushing in, he watched.

For many days, he simply watched. He sat at the back of the classroom, took notes, and listened, not just to me, but to the rhythm of the students, the silences between their words, the way they hesitated before speaking. After class, we sat and talked, first in English, then slowly in Korean. He asked what I thought the students needed, how they learned best, what worried me about the new textbooks. He never interrupted. He listened deeply.

I had worked with many people before, but this was different. He made me feel that my voice mattered. Even when we disagreed about teaching methods, he always asked me to explain more. I found myself thinking harder—about my students, about language, even about my own country. Listening, I learned, is not just waiting to speak. It is a form of respect.

That American teacher taught me that. And because of him, I became a better teacher, not just of English, but of people.

LEADERSHIP TAKEAWAYS

Listen Deeply

In international business, leaders often underestimate how much they miss, not from a lack of intention, but because they haven't learned to listen across cultures.

Peace Corps volunteers in Korea didn't only hear different languages; they entered environments where silence, tone, gesture, and even silence spoke volumes.

- **What is unsaid matters.** Learn to read between the lines in high-context cultures.
- **Listening builds trust.** Humble, patient listening signals respect and commitment.
- **Listening is cultural.** Recognize that different cultures communicate and listen in distinct ways.
- **Informal insights are gold.** Pay attention to offhand remarks, quiet moments, and subtle cues.

BOTTOM LINE: Listening deeply isn't only polite, it reflects strategic leadership.

Transition from Listen Deeply to Lead Lightly

Having honed our ability to truly hear and understand, we now face a pivotal shift: moving from *Listen Deeply* to *Leading Lightly*. *Lead Lightly* is about using what we've learned not to dominate, but to guide with humility and grace.

When we *Listen Deeply*, we understand context, culture, and connection—it becomes clear that our role as leaders isn't to command from above but to support from within. When we *Lead Lightly*, we step in where we're needed and step back when it's appropriate, trusting others to shine.

This approach honors the wisdom we've gleaned and the relationships we've nurtured. It transforms understanding into empowerment, creating space for others to lead—with our presence, not our imprint.

Chapter 3

LEAD LIGHTLY

Leadership in global development is often mistaken for control, charisma, or command. Yet, when immersed in a host culture with its own long-standing traditions, history, and rhythms, a leader quickly learns that the most powerful influence may come not from standing at the front, but from stepping back. To *Lead Lightly* is not to shrink from responsibility, but to engage differently; with humility, empathy, and the wisdom to recognize that lasting impact often emerges from the quietest moments.

This truth resonated daily during my years in Korea. We were not simply managing volunteers and programs; we were navigating the legacy of a sixteen-year bilateral partnership between the United States and the Republic of Korea, honoring the dignity of our Korean counterparts, and stewarding the sunset of a historic chapter.

My role was not to run the show but to steward its conclusion with grace, cultural humility, and steadfast care. I came into this role not to lead loudly, but to guide with a gentleness that honored the spirit of the Peace Corps and the heart of the Korean people.

The following is a reflection on a leadership principle I came to understand during this unique chapter of my life—*Lead Lightly:* a philosophy grounded in humility, deep listening, and creating the conditions for others to thrive without us taking center stage.

In Korea, a country where harmony, face-saving, and understated dignity carry great value, this leadership quality was necessary. Korea taught me that to lead lightly will carry the day in almost all situations. I learned early on that it was a style I needed to learn, and quickly.

The first group of volunteers first arrived in Korea in 1966, a decade after the Korean War, when the country was still rebuilding from devastation. Bombed-out cities were being restored brick by brick; rural areas bore deep scars—economic, emotional, and physical.

Amid this landscape of recovery, Peace Corps Korea quickly became a cornerstone of US–Korea people-to-people engagement. Volunteers taught English in rural schools, teacher colleges, and universities, while also supporting health initiatives in clinics and leprosy villages. It's important to note that they lived in communities where they were often the first foreigners residents had ever met. For many Koreans, their memories of the Peace Corps were both personal and profound. They spoke of volunteers who became part of their families—who lived with them, ate with them, celebrated their festivals, and mourned their losses. The impact was not just in the services provided, but in the human connections formed.

One middle school principal in Jeollanam-do recalled how a volunteer spent Chuseok with their family for three straight years, helping to prepare rice cakes and bowing alongside elders during ancestral rites. "He didn't just visit," she said. "He belonged." The volunteer spoke limited Korean at first, but he learned through doing, while kneading dough, laughing at his mistakes, and staying late to help clean. Her children called him *hyung,* the way one would address an older brother. Decades later, they still keep his photo in their family album.

Another story came from a retired teacher in Chungcheongbuk-do who remembered how the school's Peace Corps volunteer brought warmth into a cold cement classroom. During the winter of 1974, when fuel was scarce and students shivered in their coats, she sewed wool hand warmers for every child and handed them out one morning without fanfare. "She didn't say much," the teacher recalled, "but her actions spoke loudly. We felt cared for." Years later, that same teacher attended the volunteer's wedding in Oregon, carrying with her a gift of Korean calligraphy that read, "The heart remembers."

In a small mining town outside Taebaek, a former student remembered a volunteer who had joined the local men in repairing a collapsed bridge after heavy rains. He was muddy and exhausted as he stood shoulder to shoulder with the villagers, hauling timber and tying ropes. "He didn't just teach English," the man said. "He taught me what solidarity looked like." When he left, the entire village gathered at the bus stop to say goodbye, grandmothers bringing rice cakes, students holding hand-painted signs, miners dressed in work gear clapping and bowing.

These weren't isolated stories. Across the peninsula, memories of Peace Corps men and women endure today, not because of grand achievements, but because of small, steady gestures of a life shared. The real legacy, Koreans report, was not what the volunteers did, it was how they made people feel. Seen. Heard. Respected. Connected.

For many Koreans, the Peace Corps was more than an American program; it was a deeply human chapter in their own lives. And in those memories, the power of listening, humility, and presence continues to live on.

As the country director, I carried the responsibility of closing Peace Corps Korea's final chapter with deep respect for the legacy we shared. Though I had labored long and hard to reverse the headquarters' decision to close the program, it became my responsibility to bring about an honorable conclusion to Peace Corps Korea.

As I worked to accomplish this, I was often reminded of the importance to *Lead Lightly,* which meant honoring the past while shepherding its transition with reverence.

To *Lead Lightly* is to be present without overpowering, to guide without drawing attention to oneself. It means letting others step forward, creating room for discovery, and allowing truths to emerge on their own terms. In Korea, I learned this not from manuals or policy memos, but from quiet moments in the countryside, from walks with volunteers who were questioning everything, and from shared silences with those who simply wanted to be seen.

One of the earliest lessons I learned in Korea was the power of restraint—of silence, gestures, and what was left unsaid. Korean culture values harmony and indirect communication. Criticism, especially toward someone in authority, is rarely expressed openly. If I was to lead effectively, I needed to create space for honesty, and that meant resisting the urge to fill every silence with solutions.

I made it a point to visit volunteer sites as often as possible. Not as a supervisor checking boxes, but as a colleague willing to listen. Some of these conversations took place over kimchi stew in chilly school cafeterias; others unfolded during long walks through narrow village roads, where the mountains echoed back nothing but our footsteps. In those moments, the goal wasn't to fix anything. It was to be present.

In Gangwon-do, I visited a volunteer who taught at a girls' middle school perched above a frozen river. The school was barely heated. Students wore padded coats indoors. That afternoon, I joined her English club. The girls practiced tongue twisters and asked hesitant questions about American music. Afterward, we huddled around a kerosene stove in the teachers' office, sipping barley tea from tin cups. She spoke about her frustrations—how her co-teacher rarely let her lead, how she sometimes felt like a decorative presence. Then she shared a note a student had left her: "When you speak slowly, I feel brave."

That note captured something profound: that influence isn't always visible. Sometimes it lives in tone, patience, and presence.

In Gyeongsangbuk-do, a second-year volunteer met me at the train station with two bikes—his and a borrowed one. We rode through the rice fields glistening with spring rain. Over a modest meal with his host family, he told me how he'd stopped trying to reform the curriculum and started asking students about their dreams. That week's lesson: letters to their future selves. One read: "I want to be a teacher like our volunteer. He smiles even when I get things wrong."

Sometimes my visits felt less like oversight and more like a pilgrimage—a chance to witness the courage it took to serve in unfamiliar terrain. In Jeollanam-do, a volunteer had become part of her host community—nursing her host mother through illness, planting peppers with a neighbor, organizing a storytelling night in the town's tiny community center. Her host father poured me a cup of makgeolli and said, "You sent us a teacher, but she became our family."

Not all visits were easy. In Taebaek, I met a volunteer who had recently lost a student in a tragic accident. We walked to the school in silence. At the gate, he paused and said, "I thought I came here to teach English. But some days, it feels like I came to learn how to stand beside people in their pain."

That is what it means to lead lightly—to bear witness, to show up even when there's nothing to say.

Not every volunteer was thriving. Some wrestled with loneliness or questioned whether their efforts mattered. But the act of showing up, sitting on the floor, drinking lukewarm tea, and saying, "Tell me what it's really like," made all the difference. It said, "You matter."

The same applied to my work with Korean officials and community leaders. Some were emotional about the program's end; others were matter-of-fact. I learned to ask open-ended questions and let the pauses stretch. Often, the most heartfelt responses came when the conversation seemed over.

At one meeting, a village elder sat quietly throughout. After the formalities ended, he reached for my hand and whispered, "Please don't forget us." His grip was strong. His eyes were wet. Mine were too.

That moment became a touchstone. It reminded me that the core of leadership—especially in cross-cultural settings—is not control or charisma. It's care. To *Lead Lightly* is to carry others' hopes with humility.

As Peace Corps Korea neared closure in 1981, the emotional weight deepened. We organized farewell events, not just to commemorate accomplishments, but to hold space for collective memory. There were photo exhibits, story circles, final performances by volunteers and students, and letters read aloud that left rooms in silence.

We worked closely with our Korean staff, many of whom had been with the program from the beginning. Their insight, grace, and cultural fluency shaped every major decision. When it came time to plan final events, I asked them to lead. They did so in a way that honored both Korean tradition and Peace Corps ideals.

Leadership in that moment required subtle diplomacy, compassion, and the courage to let others lead.

Being the last country director for Peace Corps Korea was a profound privilege. It taught me that leadership is not about visibility but about presence. Not about having the answers, but about knowing when to be quiet and let others speak.

To *Lead Lightly* is to plant seeds you may never see bloom, but to trust that they will.

To explore self-reflection and practical exercises on "Lead Lightly," see the **Leadership Practice Guide** *in the back of the book.*

A Korean Voice

Dr. Shin
*Former Clinic Director, Leprosy Settlement Village,
Gyeongsangbuk-do (early 1970s)*

I had been trained as a doctor. I understood leprosy. I knew how to diagnose, prescribe, and even perform surgeries. But I now realize I did not treat my patients as people—not fully.

When the Peace Corps volunteer arrived, I thought he was naive. He was not a doctor. He spoke poor Korean. What could he possibly offer here?

But he didn't come with big ideas or demands. He came with his presence.

He sat beside patients others avoided. He played with children whose parents were hidden away. He learned each name, not just the disease.

He asked me about protocols, but more often he asked, 'What do the patients want?' I didn't know how to answer. I had never asked.

Once, I saw him holding the hand of an elderly man whose fingers had long since disappeared. They were laughing—not about anything important, just about a misused Korean phrase. But the sound of that laughter changed something in me.

The volunteer never gave me a lecture. He never told me to change. But watching him...I began to see the shame I had carried—the fear that if I got too close, I would lose something.

Instead, he showed me what I had already lost: compassion.

By the time he left, I was a different kind of doctor. I had learned to see again.

That young American never led loudly. But his gentleness—his quiet conviction—led all of us.

LEADERSHIP TAKEAWAYS

Lead Lightly

Leadership isn't about being the loudest voice in the room—it's about exercising strength with humility, illuminating others without dimming their light. In Peace Corps Korea, the most enduring leaders were those who led gently, creating space for others to grow and shine.

- **Empower through quiet guidance.** Stepping in briefly to support—then stepping back—creates space for trust and ownership to flourish.
- **Observe before acting.** A softly spoken directive, grounded in deep awareness, goes farther than grand commands.
- **Let go of control.** As Kevin O'Donnell reminded us, *My biggest job...was to get the hell out of the way.* True leadership trusts the process of local growth.
- **Cultivate shared leadership.** Invite volunteers, local staff, and community members to lead alongside you. Both service and legacy depend on collective action.

BOTTOM LINE: To lead lightly isn't a sign of weakness; it's a demonstration of deep strength and a belief in the collective. By holding lightly with one hand, we lift firmly with the other.

Transition from Lead Lightly to Trust Wisely

When we *Lead Lightly*—stepping forward to support and stepping back to empower—we nurture environments where confidence, creativity, and ownership can flourish. This kind of leadership asks us to center others, to recognize that true guidance often happens in subtlety, not spectacle.

But gentle leadership is only the beginning. To build something lasting, we must take the next step and *Trust Wisely*. That means making the deliberate choice to entrust responsibility, to place decision-making power where understanding and commitment lie, and to balance belief in others with prudent oversight.

Trust Wisely is not naive. It doesn't mean letting go without vigilance. Instead, it invites us to set clear expectations, offer support, and hold ourselves—and others—accountable with grace. In that space, leadership becomes a partnership, strengthened by mutual belief and shared responsibility.

Chapter 4

TRUST WISELY

Leadership is often measured by vision, decisiveness, and authority, but beneath all of this is a quieter, more powerful force: trust. Without trust, no vision can be realized, no decision accepted, and no authority respected. In the context of Peace Corps Korea, trust was not simply a leadership trait; it was a daily practice, a mutual agreement, and a bridge across differences. For Americans serving as volunteers and staff, and for Koreans welcoming these strangers into their schools, clinics, and homes, trust was the invisible thread that made the entire endeavor possible—quietly stitching together the daily moments that turned service into connection.

From the perspective of a country director, I recognized that trust was not granted by position. It had to be earned in a thousand small moments: in how we listened, how we responded, how we showed up. Trust was rooted in integrity, consistency, and humility.

This chapter explores trust in the context of Peace Corps Korea: its policies, its people, and the countless quiet acts that made lasting impact possible.

Arriving Without a Net

When the first group of Peace Corps volunteers arrived in Korea in 1966, they entered a country still rebuilding after a devastating war. Electricity flickered inconsistently in rural areas, if it existed at all. Infrastructure was limited. Many of the roads were still unpaved, and many of the towns volunteers lived in had never hosted a foreigner.

Imagine being age twenty-three, barely out of college, landing in Seoul with two suitcases, a few months of language training, and a mission to teach English, assist in health clinics, and support community development in a place you barely understood. There were no smartphones, no instant translations, no GPS. Volunteers had to place their trust in their host counterparts, their Korean neighbors, and their own ability to learn.

Just as crucially, Korea had to trust them.

Teachers, principals, local government officials, and host families welcomed these young men and women into their lives with open arms...but also with cautious hearts. Despite the fact that the Cold War context made every foreigner a potential object of suspicion, trust took root.

Volunteers were met at train stations by curious children and cautious elders. In some villages, people lined the streets just to catch a glimpse of the foreigners who had come so far. The first impressions were powerful, and often, bewildering. Volunteers arrived with western clothing, books, and notions of pedagogy, but were quickly humbled by the realities of rural Korean life: outhouses, coal briquettes for heat, unfiltered well water, and the communal rhythm of village life.

"I remember arriving at my placement in North Gyeongsang Province," one volunteer recalled, "and seeing my name written in Hangul on the school gate. The principal had made a sign: 'Welcome Teacher Robert.' That sign told me everything. I was wanted here. Even before I opened my mouth, they were reaching out."

That reaching out, that act of welcome, wasn't always easy. Korea in the late 1960s was a place of resilience and pride, but also of memory, of colonial rule, of civil war, of division. Many Koreans had never spoken to an American. For older generations, Americans were both liberators and reminders of past chaos. And yet, these communities opened their homes, their meals, and their lives to these young strangers.

At the same time, volunteers were expected to adapt, not be catered to. There were no special allowances for food preferences or creature comforts. Volunteers bathed in cold water, ate kimchi with every meal, and navigated chopsticks as best they could. They were laughed at, corrected, and sometimes misunderstood. But they were also taught, invited, and slowly, deeply, accepted.

One early volunteer was placed in a mountainous village near Chuncheon. Her house was a single room with paper walls and a wood floor. Her school had no heating system. During winter months, she wore three sweaters to class and kept her ink bottles in a sock to prevent freezing. Yet, she spoke of those days with reverence.

"I was cold, yes, but never alone. The students would bring me roasted chestnuts from their homes. The vice principal gave me a hot water bottle made from an old whiskey flask. The teachers invited me to their homes, and even though I understood maybe twenty percent of the conversation, I knew I belonged."

This sense of belonging didn't come from a perfect cultural fit. It came from effort—from the visible, humble, awkward, daily steps volunteers took to integrate. They knelt at meals even when their knees ached. They practiced Korean verbs late into the night. They wrote letters home filled with confusion and hope.

And through those efforts, they weren't just noticed—they

were accepted. Seen not as guests or foreigners, but as people trying, sincerely, to belong.

One school janitor was overheard telling a student, "That young American teacher, he bows lower than the vice principal." It was not about deference; it was about respect. Koreans noticed. They appreciated it. And they responded.

In small ways, trust was offered and returned. In the springtime, a student's father might invite a volunteer to help plant rice. A neighbor might drop off extra pickled radish or soybean paste. A principal might allow the young teacher to conduct an English song lesson, even if it defied conventional curriculum. These gestures built a network of mutual appreciation that transcended language and social customs.

Another volunteer served in a fishing village on the southern coast. His first weeks were isolating. He found the dialect difficult and the local men distant. One evening, as he walked home from school, he saw a group of older men sitting under a pavilion drinking makgeolli, a sparkly rice wine. One man beckoned him over. "Sit," he said in Korean. He sat. They passed him a cup. No words needed. Just presence.

From that evening forward, he was part of the community. He was invited to weddings, funerals, and fishing trips. He said later, "They taught me how to gut a fish, how to tie a net, and how to listen without interrupting. I learned more about peace building from those men than any university could offer."

Even in moments of failure or embarrassment, trust was able to grow. Volunteers who accidentally offended were often corrected gently, not rejected. That was because the Koreans valued intention. They understood that these young Americans were trying, that they had come not as tourists, but as participants.

"I once wore shoes inside the classroom," recalled a volunteer. The janitor looked horrified. But instead of yelling, he gently took me aside and showed me how to clean the floors with a rag tied to my feet. We did it together. We didn't share a language, but we shared a moment."

Arriving without a safety net meant relying on the kindness of strangers and discovering that strangers can become family. It meant navigating bureaucracy in a foreign language, accepting mistakes as teachers, and finding joy in simplicity. It meant realizing that maps were less important than relationships.

Many volunteers carried a valuable lesson long after they left Korea: true connection does not require perfection, only effort and humility.

As one staff member put it, "We asked these young people to enter the unknown, to go beyond the reach of American comfort, and to do so with grace. They arrived unprepared in many ways, but they came with open hearts. And Korea met them there."

This was not charity. It was not rescue. It was not adventure tourism. It was service and mutual discovery.

Our volunteers may have arrived unprepared, but what they found was a woven tapestry of humanity—fragile, flawed, and beautiful—that held them as they learned, stumbled, and grew.

And that, perhaps more than any formal training or orientation, was the beginning of real trust.

Don Hess, the second country director of Peace Corps Korea, demonstrated the profound trust he had in Korea. He bucked the Peace Corps trend by initiating host-country training, "trust isn't just given—it's cultivated through shared responsibility and lifted by the confidence we place in others."

Trust as Policy: *The Host Country Request Model*

One of the foundational elements of the Peace Corps model that fostered trust was the requirement that host countries request volunteers. This was done to accentuate our belief that we never wanted to be seen as a program that imposed itself on its hosts. Korean schools, ministries, and health offices had to articulate their needs, outline roles, and prepare specific rules and program expectations before they could receive the volunteers.

This initial posture of being invited, rather than giving the appearance of invading, created a baseline of respect. It framed the relationship as a partnership. It also placed Korean institutions in the lead role which, in turn, created a trust that grew from ownership.

Years later, a former high school principal from Gangwon Province remarked, "When I heard Americans were coming to teach English, I thought, why would they come here, to our mountain village? But then I saw that they stayed. That they tried. That they respected our way. And then I trusted them."

This quote illustrates a deeper truth, one that proved the Host Country Request Model wasn't theoretical or administrative. It was lived. It had roots in the way Korea defined self-determination. After enduring occupation, war, and deep structural rebuilding, Korea in the 1960s was not just seeking outside help; it was choosing its partners. And this act of choosing was itself a declaration of sovereignty.

The Host Country Request Model also created a sense of accountability that flowed both ways. Korean government offices, particularly the Ministry of Education and the Ministry of Health and Social Affairs, had to be clear about their goals and expectations. They had to define roles for the volunteers, roles that aligned

Trust Wisely

with national priorities and local capabilities. This planning process encouraged Korean leaders and community partners to think strategically and holistically about how best to utilize this unique foreign assistance. Volunteers were not seen as parachuting into the country to solve undefined problems. They were seen as men and women incorporated into systems already in place, and in roles shaped by the Koreans.

In practice, this led to a more meaningful integration and less resistance. When Peace Corps Korea staff met with local educational boards or health officials during the placement process, these meetings weren't abstract. They were detailed, collaborative, and rooted in the realities that existed in the country. Our Korean partners were candid about the challenges they faced, and this honesty created a place in which volunteers could be matched with communities where they were genuinely needed.

There's a story from 1971, when a rural school in North Gyeongsang Province requested a volunteer to teach English. The headmaster was known for his meticulous planning. He submitted an application to the Ministry outlining not just a need for English instruction, but also a community support plan. That included a host family willing to take in a volunteer, a budget to provide supplemental teaching materials, and a clear outline of shared responsibilities between the volunteer and Korean teachers. When the volunteer, a young woman, arrived, she found herself immediately welcomed, not because she was a foreigner, but because she had been asked for.

The headmaster later wrote in a letter to Peace Corps staff, "Our school did not receive a stranger. We received a partner. And the reason is because we chose to."

That spirit of mutual agreement also extended to the way

communities evaluated and supported volunteers. In many cases, local officials and principals took personal responsibility for the success of the partnership. They did not merely tolerate the presence of a foreigner...they felt a stake in the volunteer's well-being and integration. When tensions arose, as they sometimes did, over cultural misunderstandings or workload expectations, these were often resolved, not through top-down orders, but through dialogue between equals.

This framework also meant that our Peace Corps staff had to operate differently. Rather than assigning volunteers based on availability or logistics, they worked to align individual skills with specific community requests. That required a deep understanding of local conditions, institutional culture, and long-term goals. It required staff to travel, to listen, and to ask more than tell.

And it required that they truly knew each volunteer—not just their résumés, but their personalities, strengths, and capacity to adapt. Assignments were made not just by qualifications, but by character and fit.

I recall a former Peace Corps Korea Program officer's description of a visit to a small teacher's college in Chungcheong Province. The dean of the English department asked pointed questions about curriculum goals, classroom methodology, and the potential for long-term collaboration. He was not interested in a symbolic appointment. He wanted to bring in a professional. "We request not a visitor," he said, "but a teacher who will grow with us."

This attitude revealed something profound: trust was not built on blind enthusiasm, but on realism, preparedness, and shared purpose. By inviting Korean institutions to define their own needs, Peace Corps wasn't simply offering assistance—it was respecting sovereignty. That acknowledgment was powerful. In later years, many of these same institutions—schools, hospitals, local governments—would go on to launch their own international partnerships. Some even hosted volunteers from other countries. The model had planted a seed. Not just of trust, but of how to structure and sustain that trust.

That kind of reciprocity mattered. It still does.

Trust in the Classroom: *A Two-Way Street*

Teaching is one of the most intimate and vulnerable of professions. It requires presence, authority, empathy, and a constant awareness of others' perceptions. For Peace Corps volunteers, it also required adaptation. Korean students were accustomed to memorization, discipline, and clear hierarchies. Volunteers brought something different. They introduced conversation, creativity, and personal engagement.

That cultural clash could have easily backfired, but an established trust opened the door.

Take the story of a volunteer from Ohio who taught in a boys' middle school in Daegu in 1972. His students were rigid, quiet, and initially intimidated by his height and foreignness. He sensed their fear, so he began spending time outside the classroom. He joined after-school clubs, helped clean the grounds, and learned their dialect phrases. One day, he overheard a group of students referring to him not as *yangnomo*, a slang word for foreigner, but as *uri seonsaengnim, our teacher.* That subtle shift marked a turning point. He had built trust not through lessons, but through presence. From that moment, the classroom came alive.

One of the volunteers was assigned to a girls' high school in Jeonju in 1975. She arrived eager to engage her students in conversation practice. But her enthusiasm quickly met a wall of silence. The students were polite, even deferential, but they rarely responded beyond *yes* or *no*. She confided in her Korean co-teacher, who advised patience and offered insight: "They're not shy," she explained. "They're worried about disappointing you." She responded by shifting her approach. She created games, wrote dialogues based on K-drama plots, and let her students direct classroom activities. She also shared pieces of her own life, family photos, handwritten letters from home, simple stories of her Midwestern upbringing. One day, a student stayed behind after class and handed her a note written in careful English: "I want to be a teacher like you. Because you see us." Her trust in her students' potential allowed them to trust in themselves. And in her.

Another layer of classroom trust emerged in teacher training colleges, where volunteers were assigned to work with future educators teaching English. These settings offered a rare opportunity for systemic impact. Volunteers were not only shaping students but also influencing the next generation of Korean teachers.

One of the volunteers was a linguistics graduate and assigned to a teachers' college in Busan in 1978. He collaborated with the Korean faculty to develop pronunciation workshops and communicative grammar sessions. Early on, the Korean professors were skeptical of his less structured approach, so he invited them to observe and participate, even offering to co-teach select lessons. Over months, a mutual respect grew. One professor later said, "We did not trust the method, but we trusted the man." Together, they published a bilingual resource manual for rural English teachers, combining Peace Corps strategies with Korean pedagogical norms. That manual was still in circulation years after the program ended.

Volunteer-led English language workshops for Korean teachers also became a cornerstone of trust-building. These workshops, often held during school breaks or at provincial education offices, brought together Korean teachers, who were eager to improve their spoken English, and volunteers who had learned how to teach not just with textbooks, but with authenticity and adaptability.

One such workshop, organized in Gyeongsangbuk-do in 1977, drew over fifty Korean teachers. Led by four Peace Corps volunteers, it focused on conversational fluency, pronunciation, classroom games, and cultural exchange. The Korean teachers were shy at first, concerned about errors or embarrassment. But the volunteers created a space of warmth and laughter. Mistakes were met with encouragement. Questions were welcomed.

At the closing ceremony, one Korean teacher stood up and said, "Before, I taught English like math. Now, I see it as music. Alive. Shared."

These workshops seeded more than language skills. They seeded professional friendships, mutual respect, and a vision of collaboration. The volunteeers were often invited back to schools months later to observe classes, consult on lesson plans, or even co-teach special sessions. In doing so, they became not just instructors but trusted colleagues.

In a country that deeply values education and reveres teachers, to be accepted as a trusted educator was one of the highest honors a Peace Corps volunteer could earn. And it didn't happen automatically. It happened through persistence, humility, cultural learning, and genuine affection.

Health Volunteers: *Trust and Vulnerability*

Perhaps nowhere was trust more necessary, and more delicate, than in the work of Peace Corps health volunteers. These men and women worked in rural clinics, midwifery centers, and small public health outposts where resources were minimal and cultural practices deeply rooted.

One of the volunteers was stationed in a coastal town in South Jeolla in 1969. She remembered how patients initially refused to be seen by her. They would wait for the Korean nurse, even if it meant waiting all day. Rather than push herself into the center, she asked the local nurse to let her assist quietly. She washed linens. She boiled water. She asked questions. Slowly, patients began to accept her presence.

One elderly woman, who had refused treatment for a persistent infection, finally let her change her bandages. Through a translator, the woman explained, "Because you waited with me, I believe you care."

Her medical knowledge was not the key; her patience was. And from that moment, she was trusted.

Another example comes from a volunteer who was assigned to a remote leprosy treatment village near Gwangju in the early 1970s. When he arrived, the community had already faced decades of isolation and stigma. Most of the residents lived in simple cottages clustered around a small clinic. The Korean health workers were dedicated but overburdened. The Peace Corps member's presence was met at first with wary eyes and silence. Rather than launch into new initiatives or attempt to take charge, he did something rarely seen: he spent the first weeks sweeping floors, organizing supplies, and learning everyone's names. He played with the children, who were initially shy but curious. He shared his lunch, accepted invitations to sit, and respected the rhythm of the village.

One afternoon, a resident invited him to his home. Over barley tea, he asked, "Why would someone like you come to live among us?"

"Because I believe you deserve the same dignity and care as anyone else," he said. "And because I want to learn from you."

From that day, the village began to open up. He helped repair roofs damaged in monsoon rains and taught basic first aid to younger residents. He assisted with the delivery of food and medicine during shortages. Over time, he became not a visitor, but a neighbor.

Years later, he returned during a Korea Foundation Revisit Program. The resident, now an elder with limited mobility, greeted him with tears. "You didn't just treat our wounds. You saw our humanity. That's what healed us."

Stories like these are not exceptions. During our time in Korea, they were the quiet norm. In clinics and rural health posts throughout Korea, members of the Peace Corps learned to surrender assumptions and lean into humility. Trust, after all, was never guaranteed. It was earned over long hours, through respecting silence, and in posing questions rather than giving answers.

I'm reminded of a midwife volunteer in North Gyeongsang Province in 1971. She was placed at a women's health center where childbirth was deeply rooted in tradition. Many women feared hospitals, and birthing took place at home, often aided by mothers, grandmothers, or *sanhujorisa*, local birth attendants. Our midwife knew her training from the US would mean little if she did not first listen. She shadowed the attendants, learned how they read the mother's pulse and how they used herbal compresses. She also learned how they prayed over the newborn.

Only after many months was she asked to assist during a home birth. That day, she and the sanhujorisa worked side by side. After the baby was born, the grandmother of the house pressed her hand and said, "You didn't come to teach us. You came to learn with us. That is why we trust you."

There was vulnerability, too, on the part of our volunteers. Illness, isolation, and emotional strain often visited them. In these moments, it was Korean doctors, nurses, and neighbors who became caregivers. Trust flowed both ways. One volunteer recounted being hospitalized for appendicitis and waking to find his Korean supervisor sleeping in the chair next to his bed. "He didn't go home until I was out of danger. That's not just kindness, that's family."

As trust grew, so did the scope of the work. Volunteers were often asked to take on responsibilities beyond what they had expected. This included running immunization drives, helping to build sanitation systems, or training new health workers. But even in these expanded roles, the ethos remained: to listen, to learn, to serve.

Looking back, many Korean health professionals credit the Peace Corps with sparking shifts in rural healthcare, not because they brought superior knowledge, but because they brought a different spirit. Collaboration replaced hierarchy. Empathy took root alongside expertise. And the idea that healthcare was not just a service but a relationship began to grow.

This transformation didn't happen overnight. It happened over years of showing up, of staying quiet when needed, of advocating when it mattered. It happened in the slow weaving of trust, thread by thread.

Today, many of those small rural clinics have become modern hospitals. The once-isolated leprosy villages have integrated into broader society. And in some of those places, a photograph still hangs on the wall of a young American in a Peace Corps windbreaker, laughing with children, tending to a patient, or sitting in the shade of a courtyard with elders.

Trust, once a fragile seed, had grown into memory. And that memory, passed down in stories and gestures, continues to nourish the values of shared care, humility, and dignity.

Health volunteers didn't provide only services. By being respectful, they modeled what it meant to be invited into another's world. They showed that vulnerability could be strength. That presence was power. That trust, when given, could heal more than bodily wounds.

This legacy endures not only in the improved health systems, but in the hearts of those who remember. And in the generations who continue to believe that even across language and culture, true care is always understood.

Trust Among Volunteers: *Building a Culture*

Trust also had to live within the Peace Corps community. Volunteers came from diverse backgrounds—rural farms, Ivy League schools, activist circles, conservative households. When they gathered for training or mid-service conferences, they brought all those perspectives and experiences with them.

The country director and staff had to create a culture where those differences could coexist, where respect was practiced and expected. I remember one volunteer who struggled deeply with the hierarchy embedded in the Korean classroom. He felt it conflicted with his egalitarian values. He resisted using titles. He corrected Korean teachers. Conflict was inevitable. But instead of correcting him, we invited conversation. We paired him with another volunteer who had thrived in the Korean system. Over time, he learned that trust didn't require abandoning his values, it required honoring others'. He learned to use *seonsaengnim* (teacher) not as a symbol of oppression, but a sign of cultural fluency. His classroom blossomed.

These internal trust-building moments were just as critical as the work the volunteers did outside. For many, the Peace Corps was their first experience living in close quarters with people radically different from themselves. Dormitory-style housing during training in Chuncheon or Suwon meant shared bathrooms, late-night debates, and communal frustrations. The stress of cultural immersion, language fatigue, and isolation could either fracture the group or forge bonds of steel.

One of the volunteers came from rural Texas, and her roommate during training was a Jewish activist from New York. Their initial relationship was fraught with misunderstanding. The Texan found the New Yorker too brash; the New Yorker found the Texan too reserved. But one humid night after language class, the Texan shared a story about her grandmother teaching her how to plant vegetables by the moon's cycles. Her roommate listened, intrigued. That conversation led to more about faith, family, and justice. By the end of the training, they were each other's fiercest protectors.

One of our mid-service conferences was held in Busan, and I recall a particularly tense moment during a session on gender equity. A male volunteer interrupted a female colleague to question her account of harassment. The room froze. Before I could speak, another volunteer stood up, not with anger, but with clarity and said, "We all came here to serve Korea, but we also need to serve each other. That means believing each other's pain."

That moment changed the tone of the entire conference. It wasn't about shame. It was about accountability and trust. The volunteer who spoke out later became a peer mentor to incoming volunteers who was known and respected for his listening ear and steady presence.

That culture of trust became one of our greatest strengths. It meant that when volunteers needed help, they didn't hesitate to reach out. It meant that when someone faltered, others picked up the slack. It meant that even decades later, those bonds endured.

Today, I think of that culture as one of the most beautiful legacies of Peace Corps Korea. It didn't emerge from perfect harmony or shared ideologies. It emerged because people chose to trust, again and again, across differences, across silences, across time.

Crisis and Trust: *The Assassination of President Park*

In October 1979, Korean President Park Chung-hee was assassinated. The country entered a period of political upheaval, uncertainty, and fear. Martial law was declared. Protests flared. Curfews were imposed. Foreigners were watched more closely.

For Peace Corps Korea, this was a test of trust on every level.

Volunteers called the office with questions, fears, and rumors. Families back home panicked. The US Embassy issued vague advisories. It would have been easy to retreat, to suspend the program.

But we didn't.

Instead, we called every volunteer. We explained what we knew and what we didn't. We offered reassurances only where we could be honest. We asked for their trust, and we gave them ours.

And not one volunteer asked to go home.

They trusted the Peace Corps staff. They trusted their Korean communities. One volunteer wrote, "I realized that if something happened, my Korean host family would protect me before I even knew there was danger. That's trust. That's love."

The Gwangju Uprising

Just months later, in May 1980, that fragile trust was again tested, perhaps even more severely, with the eruption of the Gwangju Uprising. What began as student-led demonstrations against martial law in the southern city of Gwangju turned into a brutal and tragic confrontation between citizens and the military. The government's response was swift and violent. Estimates of those killed range from several hundred to over a thousand, many of them students and civilians.

At the time, Peace Corps Korea had several volunteers stationed in or near the Jeolla provinces. Communication lines were cut. Curfews became stricter. Some volunteers were confined to their homes or schools by concerned Korean hosts. Others watched as tanks rolled through the streets.

One volunteer was assigned to a teacher's college just outside Gwangju. She later recounted how one of her Korean colleagues quietly pulled her aside and said, "You must stay inside today. Bad things are happening. Please trust me." She obeyed without question, although she didn't fully understand. But she felt the tension in the air and she trusted her colleague. The college emptied. Roads were blocked. Rumors flew.

In the days that followed, several volunteers near Gwangju became silent witnesses to the aftermath. They saw grieving families. They heard whispers of missing students. But most critically, they respected the silence that was required at the time. This was not a silence of indifference, but of solidarity.

One health volunteer remembered going to work the week after the crackdown. The clinic staff wore black ribbons. No one spoke of what had happened. When he asked if he could help in any way, a senior nurse placed a hand on his shoulder and said, "Just stay. Just do your work. That is how you help."

That was the theme echoed across Peace Corps Korea during that dark time. Stay. Do your work. Be present.

For many volunteers, Gwangju became a lesson in humility. It revealed the limits of what they could understand as outsiders, the risks of stepping into a nation's grief without context, and the importance of witnessing pain without making themselves the story. Years later, during revisit programs and conversations with former Korean counterparts, the events of Gwangju would come up. One Korean teacher told a returned volunteer, "You didn't ask questions. You didn't run away. You stayed. That meant more than you knew."

Trust, during a time of political violence, is not only about personal safety. It is about choosing to remain grounded in respect. It is about believing in the resilience of those around you. The Gwangju Uprising was not a chapter of Peace Corps Korea that showed up in newsletters or end-of-service reports. But in quiet ways, it shaped a generation of volunteers and deepened the trust between Americans and Koreans, men and women who had weathered something unspeakable together.

In those months between the assassination of a president and the bloodshed in Gwangju, Peace Corps Korea evolved into more than a development program. It became a human bond, a shared silence. At its core was a commitment to show up, even when the world seemed to be falling apart.

Long-Term Trust: *Returning Years Later*

In the 2000s, many former volunteers returned to Korea. For most, these journeys were deeply emotional. At the heart of these emotions was how deeply the volunteers and American staff were remembered by the Koreans. Not for their accomplishments, but for their presence.

A former volunteer shared this story: "I returned to my village in Gangwon-do. I walked up the same dirt road I had walked a hundred times in the 1970s. I didn't think anyone would remember me. But a man came running out from a small shop. He said, 'Is it you?' It was one of my students. He brought me to his home, introduced me to his grandchildren, and said, 'This is our American teacher. She never left our hearts.'"

That's trust. Not a momentary transaction, but a lifelong memory built through daily kindness, humility, and respect.

Another returnee visited the school in South Jeolla Province where he had taught English nearly thirty years earlier. The school had grown and the dirt courtyard had become a concrete sports field. The one-room teacher's lounge was now a multi-story administrative building. He expected anonymity. Instead, he was welcomed with a banner, a table of elders, and a group of students who had prepared a skit based on the stories their parents had told them about the American *seonsaengnim*.

He was overcome. "I didn't think my two years here meant anything beyond the moment. But these people, they carried it forward. They made my presence part of their family's story."

These moments were not isolated. Dozens of former volunteers described similar encounters. Some were subtle, such as a shopkeeper remembering how a volunteer had taught their son to write his name in English. Some were grand, reflected when a school renamed its library in honor of a volunteer who had helped to build it brick by brick. Whatever the story, they all shared a common thread: the trust created by Peace Corps volunteers had lingered. Presence mattered.

For many Koreans who had lived through war, displacement, and poverty, the Peace Corps represented not a charity or a foreign policy tool but a human gesture of solidarity. One retired health worker in Busan told a visiting volunteer, "You didn't come with power. You came with your hands open. That's what we remembered."

Even the Korean media took notice. Several national newspapers ran stories highlighting the Peace Corps Korea legacy. Interviews with former students and community members described the impact in terms far more personal than political. They told of the American nurse who sat by a grandmother's bedside, a teacher who helped a struggling child pass an exam, a volunteer who played soccer every afternoon with neighborhood children.

Some volunteers found that their former students had become teachers, doctors, engineers and, in one case, a member of Korea's National Assembly. When asked about his interest in public service, the former student simply replied, "My American teacher showed me what service looks like."

All of these elements are the very essence of long-term trust. It is not transactional, and it is not always visible. Instead, it is the quiet accumulation of respect, the layering of shared experiences, the daily decisions to be kind, to be present, to listen. For the Peace Corps Korea program, this trust didn't end when the program closed. It continues today, decades later, in the hearts and memories of those who lived it.

For many of us who returned, it was both humbling and healing.

We were reminded that service—when grounded in humility and mutual respect—can leave lasting impressions. We saw firsthand that our efforts, however modest they felt at the time, had contributed to a narrative of shared dignity. And that is the greatest legacy of trust: not just that it existed, but that it lasted.

Trust and Leadership: *Lessons from the Field*

As a leader within Peace Corps Korea, I learned that trust could not be mandated. It had to be cultivated.

On a very personal level, I learned that I had to trust our staff, primarily the Korean nationals who knew far more than I about local customs, politics, and educational systems. I had to trust the volunteers to be responsible, to learn, and to recover from mistakes. I had to trust our Korean partners to guide those volunteers wisely, to be honest with them, and to trust all of us enough to support the program. And most of all, I…and everyone representing the Peace Corps…had to be worthy of their trust.

That meant being transparent when things were hard. It meant admitting when I didn't know the answer. It meant protecting volunteers when bureaucracy failed them, and advocating for our Korean staff when headquarters was slow to understand local nuances. Leadership was not about being in charge… it was about being trustworthy.

It meant listening, truly listening, and not only to the words, but to the nuances behind what staff and volunteers weren't saying aloud. During one mid-service conference, I saw a pattern emerge. Volunteers from a particular province seemed withdrawn, their feedback muted. I could have dismissed this as fatigue or homesickness, but I sensed that we needed to explore this. I asked a trusted staff member to visit their schools, sit with their Korean counterparts, and learn more about the underlying thoughts and emotions. What he uncovered was a subtle but damaging dynamic.

One of the local education supervisors had been undermining our volunteers, questioning their credentials in front of students and creating an environment of discomfort. No formal complaint had been filed, perhaps out of cultural deference or fear of causing a stir. It was because of the trust we had built with our volunteers that our staff member learned the truth.

With careful diplomacy, our Korean staff engaged with the provincial education office, raised our concerns, and were ensured a shift in personnel would be made. We made it clear that we were not just protecting Americans, but a shared mission. The change in morale was palpable.

I also learned to trust silence. In Korean culture, pauses are not always discomfort; they can be respectful space. In meetings with Ministry of Education officials or provincial health leaders, I learned to resist the Western urge to fill silence with words. That patience often yielded better results.

Volunteers learned to be experts in the art of trust. When conflicts arose with Korean partners, my instinct was to mediate, but I learned that solutions weren't always needed. What *was* needed was someone who believed in the group's capacity to solve the conflict. I remember one volunteer who had been clashing with her co-teacher. I asked her what she thought would happen if she simply asked him how he was doing. Weeks later, she wrote, "It wasn't about curriculum. It was about connections. Thank you for helping me see that."

The staff meetings, the field visits, the emergency calls in the middle of the night were all opportunities to practice trust. Trust that the work we were doing mattered. Trust that despite cultural gaps, language barriers, and bureaucratic slowdowns, we were all part of something larger.

If leadership in Peace Corps Korea revealed one core lesson, it was that trust is not a static virtue. It must be shown, shared, and renewed. Every day. In every interaction. And it is the most powerful currency a leader can hold.

When Trust is Broken

Despite the profound impact that language and culture had in fostering trust, there were moments when situations went wrong. An example is when volunteers struggled with their roles. Despite their efforts, their integration into Korean society could become strained. As much as trust was built through the effort of learning the language and respecting cultural norms, all could be quickly damaged by one misunderstanding or misstep. These moments were often magnified by the heightened sensitivity to cultural differences, as well as the pressure of representing the Peace Corps and America abroad.

One instance involved a volunteer who had been working in a rural area for several months. His commitment to the project was evident, but his manner was more direct and less deferential than the local norms allowed. In Korean culture, respect for elders and authority figures is a cornerstone to their society. When the volunteer inadvertently dismissed the advice of an elder colleague in a meeting, it struck a painful chord with the local community. The elder felt disrespected, and the community, which had initially welcomed the volunteer, began to withdraw its support. The relationship between the volunteer and the community became frayed and the school withdrew its request for a volunteer for the following year, citing a breakdown in rapport. In the aftermath, this volunteer, shaken by the response, sought advice from colleagues. It was a humbling experience for him, realizing that his failure to honor the cultural norm of respect and deference was seen not as a misunderstanding, but a betrayal of the trust that had been so painstakingly built. It was clear that words alone, no matter how skillfully delivered, could not overcome the perception of a lack of respect for the deeper cultural frameworks that underpinned every interaction.

The process of healing this breach was slow and required a great deal of reflection. The volunteer apologized to the elder. He accepted the apology, while making it clear that regaining the trust of the community would take time. This interaction was a turning point in the volunteer's relationship with the community, illustrating to him how fragile trust could be. But it also underscored the resilience of relationships when nurtured with patience, humility, and understanding.

Through the humility of apology and the ongoing effort to integrate into the community in a more culturally sensitive manner, he slowly regained the trust of the local people. His actions proved his commitment. He attended more local gatherings, listened more intently, and most importantly, showed respect not only for the cultural practices, but for the people who upheld them. Over time, the wounds healed and new relationships were established, stronger than before.

This experience also highlighted a critical aspect of cross-cultural work, That is, that trust is dynamic. It is not something that is fully established and then left untouched. Instead, trust is a living, breathing entity that requires constant attention and nurturing. When it is broken, the path to restoration takes time, reflection, and sincere efforts. But trust *can* be rebuilt, not through grand gestures, but through consistent actions that demonstrate a genuine commitment to understanding and respecting others.

These lessons are not unique to the Peace Corps or to Korea. They transcend borders and cultures. They remind us that while trust may be fragile, it is also durable when nurtured with the right intentions, patience, humility, and a willingness to learn and grow.

Trust as Compass

Trust was lived daily—in the mud and the mountains, in classrooms and clinics, in tea shared and stories exchanged. It was never assumed. It had to be nurtured, tested, and earned through the smallest of gestures. For the men and women of Peace Corps Korea, trust flowed in both directions: young Americans stepping into a world they did not know, and Koreans opening that world with generosity and grace.

This daily practice of trust was woven into the fabric of every interaction. Whether it was the volunteer who stepped into a classroom, unsure of their lesson but committed to doing their best, or the doctor in a rural clinic who patiently worked with local health workers to share knowledge, trust was always present. The quiet understanding that no one was perfect but everyone was there with good intentions created an atmosphere for learning, growth, and change…some were barely discernible, while others changed lives.

At the heart of those daily acts was something deeper—trust. The trust of colleagues who built something together. The collaboration between Korean staff, local teachers, and Peace Corps volunteers became a powerful force. Together, they forged bonds that transcended differences in language, culture, and worldview. It wasn't always easy, but their shared commitment to serve—and to learn from one another—kept them united. That bond, that sense of common purpose, helped them overcome obstacles that might have seemed insurmountable in any other setting.

Trust also defined the work of Peace Corps staff, who navigated cultural, institutional, and logistical complexities every day. Operating under sometimes ambiguous circumstances, they learned that success depended not on control, but on building trust—with local communities, with volunteers, and with national counterparts. They listened, adapted, and led with integrity. More than administrators, they became mentors and cultural bridges—models of the reciprocal trust that made the Peace Corps experience possible.

The trust of communities who embraced the unfamiliar was one of the most profound aspects of the Peace Corps Korea experience. Communities, many of whom had never interacted with foreigners before, opened their doors, homes, and hearts. They welcomed the volunteers into their daily lives, not because they expected perfection, but because they saw the sincerity behind the volunteers' efforts. The volunteers became more than just temporary visitors; they became part of the community. In this embrace of the unfamiliar, Koreans demonstrated an incredible generosity of spirit and a deep belief in the power of human connection.

Volunteers didn't return to Korea because they had changed Korea, but because Korea had changed them. The trust built across language, culture, and distance endured—reflected in reunions where former volunteers were welcomed not as visitors, but as family.

In leadership, as in life, trust is not something we demand. It is something we must earn. Slowly. Patiently. Humbly. It is built over time, one action, one word, and one moment of understanding at a time. Peace Corps Korea and Koreans taught us that lesson well. Through patience, openness, and the willingness to trust us with their culture and their lives, the Korean people showed us that trust is not something given lightly. But once earned, it becomes the foundation upon which all future relationships are built. It is the lasting gift that remains, long after the formal work is done.

Explore practical exercises and reflection prompts for "Trust Wisely" in the **Leadership Practice Guide***, located in the back of the book.*

A Korean Voice

Mr. Choi
*Former Provincial Supervisor of English Education,
Gangwon-do (1970s)*

At that time, our English curriculum was rigid—focused on grammar drills, memorization, and recitation. We believed fluency came from discipline, not conversation. So, when we heard that American volunteers would be assisting in our schools, many of us were skeptical. Some principals even refused them.

But I watched.

They did not criticize our methods. They did not try to take control. They observed. They asked questions—always respectful, always curious. One volunteer in a small mountain town asked if he could visit every English teacher in the district—not to evaluate, but to understand.

He listened more than he spoke.

Over time, something changed. Teachers who had never spoken English aloud began to try. One principal invited the volunteer to speak during a faculty meeting. Another began experimenting with role-play exercises. Not all at once. But steadily.

This was not the result of pressure. It was the result of trust.

The volunteer did not demand change. He built

relationships. He showed, by example, that confidence could grow where fear once lived. That to teach a language, one must also create a space for voices.

In the end, the changes were modest. But they were real. A few new words in a classroom. A bit more laughter. A teacher staying late to practice.

In Korean schools, trust must come before permission. The volunteers understood this. They earned it, step-by-step. And in doing so, they helped open the door to a different kind of learning.

LEADERSHIP TAKEAWAYS

Trust Wisely

Trust is the foundation of every successful cross-cultural relationship. It is not granted lightly, it is built slowly through presence, humility, and consistency.

- **Trust requires proximity.** Show up. Be physically present and actively engaged in the work and with the people you serve.
- **Trust starts at a deficit.** Outsiders, regardless of intention, must earn trust patiently and through repeated acts of respect.
- **Humility beats expertise.** When you admit what you don't know and ask for guidance, you invite collaboration and demonstrate respect.

BOTTOM LINE: Without trust, no strategy, no project, and no vision can succeed. It is the silent partner in every sustainable achievement.

Transition from Trust Wisely to Lead Fiercely

When we *Trust Wisely*—placing confidence in others while maintaining clarity in expectations—we reinforce the bonds that allow leadership to take root and grow. As Doug Conant, former CEO of Campbell Soup Company and a widely respected leadership author, reminds us: "Trust starts small and gets big. It's not a nice-to-have; it's a must-have."

That foundation of trust is more than a safety net. It can be the springboard for something far stronger: hope. Courage in leadership comes not only from past reliability but from envisioning what's possible when people are empowered. The combination of trust, courage, and hope form a powerful trio leading us toward what is real and reliable...and what might lay ahead.

To *Hope Fiercely* is to lean into that possibility with conviction, even when the outcome is uncertain. It means trusting others to carry forward what you've started, even if you never see the results yourself.

II
BELIEF

Chapter 5

HOPE FIERCELY

Leadership is often seen through the lens of rational planning, strategic vision, and measured execution. But another element, equally vital and often underestimated, is hope. Hope is not passive optimism. It is not being naïve or blind to obstacles. Hope, especially fierce hope, is the willful decision to believe in what is possible despite evidence to the contrary. It is the quiet engine behind resilience, the light that keeps the road visible in darkness. During the Peace Corps Korea years, fierce hope became an everyday act of leadership practiced by volunteers, staff, and host communities.

This chapter explores how that fierce hope was forged and lived, through difficult winters, bureaucratic hurdles, cultural divides, political uncertainties, and personal transformations. It explores how we learned that to lead was to hope, fiercely, and not only in people, but in change, and in those small victories that slowly built an enduring impact.

Hope at Arrival: *Facing the Unknown*

When the first group of Peace Corps volunteers arrived in Korea, hope was immediately tested. There were no guarantees of success, living conditions were stark, and cultural misunderstandings abounded. So what kept these people rooted? What energized them to move forward? It was hope, fierce and determined hope.

One woman assigned to a rural school in Jeolla Province in 1967, wrote in her journal, "I cry some nights. The cold is sharp, and I feel so far from everything familiar. But when I teach, when I see the students trying, laughing, something stirs in me. Maybe this is what hope looks like."

Her fierce hope allowed her to stay, and it was that same hope that helped her students believe they could succeed in English, perhaps even study abroad. Hope, like trust, was contagious.

Another volunteer who was posted at a teacher training institute in Gyeongsang Province in 1968, recalled in a letter home, "I arrived with two suitcases, a Korean phrasebook, and a nervous stomach. On my first night, the water froze in my basin. I thought, 'What have I done?' But the next morning, a neighbor brought me hot tea and rice cakes, and suddenly I wasn't alone. That was the beginning of everything."

His quiet hope grew in tandem with his students' confidence, and he later led workshops across the province, helping local teachers develop their own English curricula.

One of the volunteers served in Gangwon Province in 1970. She wrote, "My school has no heating, and sometimes I can see my breath while writing on the chalkboard. But one girl, Hye-jin, comes early every day just to practice pronunciation. She tells me she wants to be an interpreter one day. That dream—it keeps both of us warm."

Her belief in small, everyday breakthroughs became the foundation for long-lasting change in her school. For her, hope was more than a feeling…it had become a habit.

Hope in Language: *Learning to Connect*

Learning Korean was a daunting task for most volunteers. The language's complexity, its honorifics, unfamiliar grammar structures, and nuanced cultural context presented steep barriers. But the effort to learn Korean wasn't just about functionality. It was a profound act of hope. To learn a language is to believe that connection is possible. To speak, however awkwardly, is to signal that the other matters enough to reach toward.

Dan Douglass, a volunteer in the mid-1970s, described his moment of linguistic breakthrough: "I was buying chestnuts from an old woman in the market. I used the wrong number marker, and she laughed so hard she nearly fell over. But she corrected me, and we talked. That conversation changed my whole relationship with that town. I wasn't just a foreigner. I was someone trying." Hope lived in those small exchanges, in the decision to risk embarrassment for the sake of understanding. Sue Cornbluth, who served in 1973 in Jeonju, recalled the first time she managed to express a complete idea in Korean: "I was trying to explain to a student why she had done well on her test. I struggled for the words, but when I finally said it, she lit up. That moment, that connection, was worth every hour of study and every moment of frustration." Likewise, Bob Hahm, who served in Chuncheon in the late 1960s, remembered a simple but profound milestone: "At first, I could only greet people. But I started keeping a little notebook with new words. One day, the school principal invited me to dinner, and I gave a short toast in Korean. The whole room applauded. I wasn't fluent, but I was understood and that meant everything."

Each phrase learned, each mistake made and corrected, was a step toward trust. In learning Korean, volunteers weren't just acquiring a skill, they were building bridges. They were expressing belief in the power of human connection. In doing so, they reminded their host communities and themselves that language is not just a tool, but a gesture of faith, respect, and enduring hope.

Hope in Classrooms: *Believing in Students*

In the 1960s and 1970s, Korean students faced immense pressure learning in a rigorous and hierarchical education system. Few had interacted with foreigners, making the arrival of the volunteer teachers a novel experience. The volunteers introduced student-centered learning that encouraged discussion, creativity, and play, all methods met with skepticism. Nevertheless, these teachers were steadfast in the hope that their students would embrace these new approaches. If they did, doors would open to new and far broader possibilities.

Alan Taylor, who taught at a middle school in Gongju from 1966 to 1968, recalled, "I've always felt that I gained more in those two turnings of the seasons in Gongju than I was able to give back. I will always feel partly Korean because of those two years." His commitment to his students went beyond academics, fostering a sense of mutual respect and understanding.

Elizabeth Fine, who taught in Jeonju from 1973 to 1975, recalled how she once asked her class to write essays about their future. One student, a quiet girl in the back row, wrote about wanting to become a writer, but assumed it was "too bold" a dream. Elizabeth said, "I told her that stories change the world. Years later, she sent me a published article. She remembered that one conversation. I had forgotten. But she hadn't."

David Kim, a Korean-American volunteer stationed in Masan in the early 1970s, shared that his Korean wasn't perfect, and some students were initially confused by a Korean face with an American accent. But that unexpected mix became its own lesson. "I told them, 'You can be both.' That idea stuck. One student later told me he went on to become an English teacher because he realized language wasn't just about speaking, it was about identity, about possibility."

In every story, one identifiable thread emerges: Peace Corps volunteers believed in their students long before those students believed in themselves. The volunteers taught more than grammar and pronunciation...they modeled curiosity, affirmation, and courage.

The sense of hope in the classroom wasn't loud or dramatic. Instead, it sounded like a volunteer pausing to listen, encouraging a student's dream, or sitting beside a shy student and saying, "I see you." In those quiet gestures, possibilities bloomed.

Hope in Health Centers

Nancy Kelly, who served in Goseong from 1979 to 1981 on a maternal-child health project, recalled how she helped deliver hundreds of babies during her service. Upon her return many years later, a good number of these babies came with their families to welcome her and thank her for her service.

Donald Grandis, who served in Wando in the late 1970s, shared a poignant moment from his revisit and the effort to search for his Korean coworker. "At the *bogeonso,* (a Korean health center) I showed them a picture of him, and they knew who it was. One of the workers called him on their cell phone, not saying why, and just handed me the phone. We instantly recognized each other's voices...it was just a moment that few people get in their life, and we were grateful for it."

Hope Among Staff: *Local Leadership and Vision*

Korean nationals who worked as Peace Corps staff were the unsung heroes of the program. They translated, mediated, coordinated, and advised. They believed in the value of the program, even when others doubted. For many, their work with Peace Corps was not just a job, it was a calling. They hoped fiercely that this cross-cultural exchange would help Korea move forward.

One of the senior education officers spent long evenings at the office helping volunteers who were struggling with lesson plans or adjusting to unfamiliar classrooms. He once told the country director, "If these young Americans are willing to travel across the ocean to teach our children, the least I can do is help them succeed." His hope was rooted in national pride and personal conviction. He believed Korea's future lay in openness, in partnership, in education.

Mr. Yi Kyung-pyo, a former Peace Corps program officer, was reunited with Donald Grandis (K-51, Wando) during the 2024 Revisit. They had not seen each other in over four decades. And yet, the bond was immediate. "We looked at each other," Grandis recalled, "and without hesitation, we hugged. The years melted away. There was something deeper than memory, it was trust. That's what we shared back then, and it was still there." Mr. Yi had been instrumental in helping volunteers navigate the expectations of local health officials and ensure safe travel to remote clinics. His quiet competence and deep care for his country's development made a lasting impression.

"He was our guide in more ways than one," said another former PCV. "Mr. Yi wasn't just scheduling site visits or tracking progress, he was showing us how to work *with* Koreans, not just for them."

Ms. Kim Jeong-sook, a bilingual secretary who worked closely with both administrative staff and volunteers, had a way of balancing the needs of both worlds. One volunteer said during the revisit, "If Peace Corps Korea was a boat, Ms. Kim was our compass. She understood us, even when we didn't understand ourselves or Korea."

Her letters to PCVs were often filled with gentle encouragement, reminders to be patient with their co-teachers, and occasional motherly nudges. "Don't forget to wear warm socks, Korean winters are no joke!" She brushed off praise. "We were all just doing our part," she said. "But I always hoped you'd leave here loving Korea just a little."

Mr. Park Seung-ho managed transportation and logistics for volunteers in Gyeongbuk Province. He was known for finding last-minute jeeps in snowstorms, sending medicine to isolated volunteers, and hand-delivering pay stubs when the postal system faltered.

"I remember calling Mr. Park in a panic when the pipes burst at my school dormitory," said a Revisit participant. "He said, 'Stay calm. I will come.' He showed up five hours later with a plumber, two blankets, and a bag of oranges."

He never sought recognition. When thanked, his response was simple: "Volunteers were far from home. I wanted them to know they were not alone."

Ms. Choi Mi-kyung was a field officer in the health program. She worked closely with nurses and sanitation volunteers. She also became, as many described her, a quiet counselor. "She never lectured. She listened," one volunteer said. "When I struggled with the sadness I felt seeing poverty I couldn't fix, she reminded me that simply being present mattered. She taught me that healing wasn't only medical, it was relational."

Ms. Choi shared how meaningful it was to see so many former volunteers return with their children and grandchildren. "I always hoped the Peace Corps legacy would live on, not just in Korea, but in your families."

What united these Korean staff members was not just professional duty, it was belief. They believed in their country's transformation. They believed in the strange, idealistic foreigners who arrived with questions and notebooks. And they believed that this collaboration could matter.

"The Peace Corps was a mirror," said Mr. Lee, who had served in both the education and agriculture programs. "We looked into it and saw Korea's potential reflected back at us. That was my hope; that working together would remind us of who we could become."

The members of the Peace Corps staff in Korea were not just interpreters of language; they were interpreters of hope. Their roles were often invisible, but they were foundational. During the 2024 Revisit, many of these people, now in their seventies and eighties, went to the welcome banquet in Seoul. Hugs, tears, laughter, and sometimes quiet, reverent silences filled the room.

One volunteer stood and said, "You believed in us before we even got off the plane. You carried us through cold winters, awkward classrooms, and missteps. We were young and clumsy. You were patient and proud. You helped us see Korea not as a hardship but as home."

The hope among staff was never loud. It was someone staying late to type a lesson plan, giving directions at a rural bus stop, or someone slipping an encouraging note into a mail pouch. These small acts were the heartbeat of Peace Corps Korea. And for every volunteer who returned decades later, that hope still echoed.

Hope Fiercely: *A Daily Practice*

I learned that hope was not a slogan. It was a discipline. It meant believing that the next placement would succeed, even if the last had failed. It meant trusting that volunteers would grow, even if they faltered. It meant defending the program when Peace Corps headquarters doubted its relevance. It meant listening when people were discouraged, and offering perspective or encouragement that helped them take the next step forward.

Hoping fiercely requires courage. But more than that, it requires a steady belief in people, in potential, in purpose. And it requires community.

Fierce hope is rarely solitary. It is nurtured in relationships—in the staff who stay late, the principals who vouch for their volunteers, the nurses who teach by example, the shopkeepers who smile at broken Korean, and the children who try, fail, and try again.

The Legacy of Fierce Hope

Peace Corps Korea ended in 1981. Its legacy continues, and not just in the memories of those who served, but in the quiet ripples of change still moving through classrooms, clinics, families, and communities.

Fierce hope is not naïve. It does not ignore the struggle. It acknowledges failure, recognizes hardship, and embraces imperfection. But it moves forward anyway.

One former volunteer, Robert Knudsen (K-35), shared: "I was twenty-four and terrified. I didn't speak the language, didn't know the culture, and was assigned to a rural middle school in North Gyeongsang Province. But my principal, Mr. Oh, came to my classroom every day, not to evaluate me, but to sit beside me, and say in halting English, 'You are doing fine. The boys like you.' He didn't have to do that. But he hoped for me until I could hope for myself."

This is the legacy of fierce hope: passed quietly, hand to hand, through moments of patience and acts of courage. Volunteers carried it. Korean staff nurtured it. And the communities, with grace and perseverance, returned it—layered with meaning, transformed into something wholly their own.

Fierce hope means showing up—again and again.

When the winter was bitter and the school dorms were unheated, teachers stayed. When health volunteers walked miles to remote clinics, they carried books, first aid kits, and dictionaries. When homesickness tried to pull them down like an anchor, they held tight to their purpose.

Hope was more than gestures. It was the daily discipline of doing the work, of showing up to the classroom even after a lesson fell flat, returning to the village clinic after a patient passed away, continuing to study Korean after making another mistake.

Marsha Fritts (K-45), a nurse volunteer in Gangwon Province, reflected: "I had no idea how to deal with tuberculosis patients when I arrived. But I had a counterpart, Nurse Jang, who believed in me. She didn't need me. But she welcomed me. She gave me a room at her house the first night. When I cried from frustration, she made kimchi pancakes and told me, 'Patience. You'll help someone, and that will be enough.' She was right."

This legacy lives not just in what the volunteers did, but in who they became. The courage they developed in Korea shaped careers, marriages, and decades of service.

As one former volunteer said, "Korea was the beginning of everything. Not because I was brave. But because I learned how to be."

Hope, practiced over time, becomes character. And that character—shaped in hanok homes, at icy bus stops, in rice fields and along mountain paths—was the quiet gift shared between Korea and the Peace Corps.

The program ended, but the friendships endured. The buildings have changed, but the impact remains.

Korean children who sat in those cold classrooms are now teachers, doctors, professors, and ambassadors. Many still remember the names of their volunteers. They remember the encouragement and the curiosity, the way someone listened to their broken English without laughing.

And they passed it on—through their own students, patients, and children—offering the same patience, respect, and quiet belief that had once been shown to them.

One Korean university professor who had been the student of a volunteer said, "He made me feel I had value. That's what stayed with me. That is why I became a teacher, to offer that same feeling to someone else."

This is the long arc of leadership: not command and control, but presence and persistence. Showing up. Listening closely. Believing deeply.

The volunteers and staff of Peace Corps Korea believed that a stranger with a notebook and a heart full of hope could make a difference. And they were right.

The world they stepped into was unfamiliar and often difficult, but they stayed. They listened and they gave. And in doing so, they were transformed—and so was Korea.

That is the legacy of leadership: *Hope Fiercely.*

Ready to explore practical exercises and journal prompts for "Hope Fiercely"? See the **Leadership Practice Guide** *in the back matter.*

A Korean Voice

Nurse Lee
Former Public Health Nurse, Tuberculosis Clinic, Gangwon-do (1970s)

Tuberculosis was a slow disease. It drained the body and the spirit. We worked with little—some medicine, old equipment, and not much hope. Many patients came alone. Some were sent by families who didn't want them at home. It was not just an illness; it was a shame. When the American volunteer arrived, I thought he would leave in a month. The work was hard, the stigma worse. But he stayed. He asked questions no one else had asked. 'What gives them comfort?' 'Who visits?' 'What did they do before they got sick?'

He started bringing small things. A harmonica for one patient. A book of Korean poetry for another. Once, he helped repaint the women's ward in light colors. He said, 'Maybe we can make it feel like somewhere worth returning to.'

It wasn't grand, but it mattered.

I saw patients who had stopped eating begin to sit up when he entered. I saw a girl who had refused her medicine asking when he would come back.

Hope is not only about curing disease. It's about reminding people that they still belong to the world.

That volunteer didn't fix everything. But he

reminded us that we were still worth effort. And in a place like ours, that was the most powerful medicine we had.

LEADERSHIP TAKEAWAYS

Hope Fiercely

Hope fuels perseverance in uncertainty. It is not simply about positive thinking; it's about fostering the resilience to keep moving forward when obstacles appear insurmountable. Leaders who inspire hope motivate their teams to overcome setbacks, to innovate, and to sustain momentum even when the results are delayed or difficult to see.

- **Celebrate progress, however small.** Recognize and honor the incremental victories. A completed project, a breakthrough idea, or even a moment of shared learning often reinforces the belief that progress is possible. This cultivates an environment where individuals feel seen and valued, and where hope is continually replenished.

- **Frame challenges as opportunities for growth.** Rather than viewing obstacles as setbacks, leaders can exhibit curiosity and creativity in facing them. By framing difficulties as learning opportunities, they encourage their teams to experiment, adapt, and continue to strive for solutions. This mindset fosters innovation and resilience.

- **Lead with optimism that is grounded, not blind.** Hopeful leadership is not naïve. It acknowledges the realities of the moment, resource limitations, cultural complexities, and shifting circumstances, but insists that possibilities remain. A leader's outlook, communicated through words, actions, and presence, shapes the team's collective spirit.

- **Show up when others hesitate.** Hope is often demonstrated in being present. Whether it's walking into a difficult meeting, visiting a struggling team member, or offering encouragement amid a crisis, a leader's willingness to stand beside others in challenging times reinforces shared purpose and a belief in the team and the future.

- **Connect hope to purpose.** Remind teams why the work matters. When the immediate outcomes are unclear, grounding hope in a shared mission helps maintain focus and commitment. In Peace Corps Korea, hope wasn't sustained by short-term results, but by a deep belief in connection, dignity, and the long arc of change.

BOTTOM LINE: Hope isn't just a concept—it's what kept me going on the hardest days. It's what I saw in the eyes of teachers who stayed after class, in students who kept trying, in staff who never gave up. Hope doesn't just inspire; it sustains. It helps us wait, rebuild, and try again. It nurtures resilience and unlocks our shared ability to imagine something better, together. The leaders I've admired most were the ones who hoped fiercely—and showed that hope not in speeches, but in how they showed up, how they listened, and how they kept believing in others, even when the path was unclear.

Transition from Hope Fiercely to Love, Always

After daring to hope—and watching that hope ripple into action—we arrive at the deepest heartbeat of leadership: *Love, Always*. Hope gives us direction; love gives us the devotion to follow through.

To *Hope Fiercely* is to plant seeds in uncertain soil—and then commit to tending them, day after day. *Love, Always* provides the patience, care, and constancy required to nurture that fragile growth. It shows up in moments of quiet support: a shared meal, an attentive ear, a hand extended with no strings attached.

Love in leadership isn't softness; it's steadfast strength. It's the courage to be present even when the work is unseen, the humility to wrap up another's sorrow, the resolve to lift others not because we lead, but because they matter.

Ultimately, love weaves through every interaction, reinforcing hope with an unshakeable bond. It transforms fleeting inspiration into enduring impact, ensuring that what we begin with conviction, we sustain with devotion.

Chapter 6

LOVE, ALWAYS

Leadership is often taught in terms of strategy, performance, and persuasion. But there is a quieter, older truth that underlies all effective leadership, particularly in intercultural service: the foundation of real impact is love. Not romantic love, nor abstract idealism, but the practical, daily expression of caring. To lead with *Love, Always*, is to approach others with deep regard, to act with generosity even when unacknowledged, and to hold steady in your commitment to the well-being of those around you.

I witnessed this form of leadership again and again. It emerged not from headquarters nor from the pages of handbooks, but from the lived experiences of volunteers, Korean staff, and coworkers who chose, despite language barriers and cultural differences and institutional fatigue, to care.

Love, Always: *Unyielding Care*

In the lexicon of leadership, we often hear about strength, strategy, and vision. Less often do we hear about love. And yet, in the context of Peace Corps Korea, a place where human connections often mattered more than programming, love was not just present, it was essential. It was expressed in long walks with students, in meals shared in silence, in the faithful presence of staff who stayed after the office lights had dimmed.

I learned that the most enduring leadership trait wasn't charisma or certainty, it was this unrelenting, quiet love. A love for people, for stories, for moments that passed without fanfare but stayed lodged in memory.

The Steady Love of Staff

The Peace Corps office in Seoul was filled with people who embodied this principle, and none more so than our Korean staff. Many had been with the program since its inception in 1966. They could recall the names of the earliest volunteers, the places they served, the communities they joined. Their institutional knowledge was invaluable, but their devotion was unparalleled.

Mr. Kim, our logistics coordinator, knew every rural road and train line, every quirk of the seasons. If any of our people were lost, sick, or confused, they could count on Mr. Kim to remain calm, kind, and capable. A blizzard stranded a volunteer in Gangwon-do, so Mr. Kim spent the night in the office calling train stations until she was located. No one asked him to do this... he did it because he cared.

Ms. Choi was our medical translator. Her gift wasn't only language fluency, but her capacity to soothe unsettled volunteers. One of them wrote that Ms. Choi's voice had calmed her more than any medicine, and that her presence in the clinic turned fear into reassurance. And not with authority, but with affection.

These acts weren't required, nor were they listed on job descriptions or measured in performance reviews. They were acts of love, an active commitment to human dignity that transcended duty.

Volunteers Who Loved, Always

Volunteers also discovered that their most lasting contributions were born not of technical skill, but of love. A health volunteer in Jeollanam-do spent months earning the trust of a leprosy village by sitting under a persimmon tree with a patient each afternoon. An English teacher in Gyeongsangbuk-do brought lunch each week for his elderly landlord. A maternal and child health worker taught prenatal care by first holding hands with expectant mothers and then walking with them to the clinic.

One former volunteer recalled, "I thought I came to teach hygiene. But what they remembered was that I carried water from the well when it froze, that I stayed when their grandmother died. That I cared."

One volunteer returned to the rural school where she had taught decades earlier. She brought a photo from 1970, her students seated in rows, their faces curious and at the same time cautious. To her astonishment, many returned to meet her, middle-aged professionals with their own children. One man had become a school principal. "You didn't just teach us English. You taught us that we mattered."

Another returning volunteer visited the family she had lived with in Jeju. They greeted her with tears, presenting a quilt made from scraps of the garments they had worn during her time there. The mother said, "You were our daughter. You are still our daughter."

But the most poignant testimonies came from Korean coworkers. Mr. Lee, who had once served as a driver, stood to speak at a dinner. "I was the one who drove you to your sites. I waited in the jeep during trainings. But I watched. I watched how you sat on floors with village elders. I watched how you waited to be invited, how you smiled even when you didn't understand. That patience, that love, it taught us about your country."

Ms. Park, a Korean language instructor, shared that she had kept every letter sent by her students, volunteers she had trained to communicate, using Korean verbs and rural dialects. "One volunteer wrote, 'I cannot conjugate properly, but I want to understand your heart.' That letter is still in my drawer."

And then there was Mr. Bae, a program officer, who said, "When Peace Corps ended, I thought the love would fade. But it didn't. It grew. Because love, when shared with humility and sincerity, becomes part of a nation's memory."

Love as a Daily Discipline

To *Love, Always* in a leadership context is not to abandon boundaries. It is to approach each decision, each conversation, each moment with reverence for the human beings involved. It is to understand that what you remember years later are not the budgets or the reports, but the people who showed up with their whole hearts.

In the field of international development, where the focus often falls on scale and measurable outcomes, this may sound quaint. But in my experience, it is precisely this ethic, this willingness to lead with love that makes real impact possible. It is what makes leadership sustainable. It is what makes service transformative.

Love, Always. It is not a soft idea. It is a radical one. One that insists that leadership without love is not leadership at all.

Volunteers and Their Host Families

Love also flourished in the bonds between volunteers and their Korean host families. In towns and villages across the peninsula, families welcomed strangers into their homes. Meals were shared, stories exchanged, and understanding of cultures and beliefs took root. There were misunderstandings, to be sure, but love persisted.

I remember one volunteer who served in Chungcheongbuk-do. She lived with an elderly couple who were skeptical of her vegetarianism and her unusual sleeping habits. But over time, they began leaving small dishes of *namul* (seasoned edible greens) without meat, and she began taking walks with them in the early morning mist. When the program ended, they cried together. She returned two years later with her newborn daughter, introducing the baby to her Korean grandparents.

During one of the Revisits held decades after the last volunteer had left, many former host families traveled to see "their Americans." Some of the Koreans carried yellowing photographs, others brought food. One woman in her eighties, walked slowly to the reunion hall carrying a bundle wrapped in faded fabric. Inside was a quilt made of old *hanbok* scraps, a gift she had meant to give her volunteer "daughter" before she left in 1973. "I didn't get the chance," she said, as she placed it in the woman's arms. "So, I saved it."

A host father from Gyeongsangnam-do stood quietly at the edge of the room until he caught sight of his volunteer. They had lived together during a time of great national uncertainty, in a village with no running water and only one working radio. "He was so skinny when he came," the man said with a laugh. "We fed him *doenjang jjigae* every day until he said he dreamed of it." When asked what he remembered most, he replied, "He listened to my son talk about his dream to become a teacher. No one else did that."

A host mother from Gangwon-do recounted how she worried the young woman assigned to her home would be too cold in the winter. "Our house was not warm. We had one small stove and many people," she said. "But she never complained. Instead, she offered to help my mother-in-law wash rice and carry coal briquettes." The memory still moved her. "She was not just a guest. She was my daughter."

Others remembered simple gestures. A family in Jeollanam-do remembered their volunteer always taking off his shoes and bowing every morning to the elders. "We thought Americans didn't understand our customs," the host sister said. "But he tried very hard. That effort stayed with us."

Although the love remained unspoken, it was lasting. A former host mother from Daegu said, "After he left, I put his picture in our family photo album. When our grandchildren asked who he was, I said, 'Your American uncle.'"

These stories, shared long after the volunteers had gone, speak to a kind of love that defies time and language. The bonds between host families and the volunteers weren't always easy, but they were lasting. They were forged in rice fields, over shared soup bowls, in rooms where words were few, but warmth was abundant.

To be welcomed into a Korean home during that era was to become part of a family, not just for two years, but for life. The Revisit Programs offered a powerful reminder that the truest legacies of Peace Corps Korea were not the projects completed or the lessons taught, but the hands held, the rooms shared, and the hearts opened—quietly, irrevocably—and with love.

Coworkers Who Became Family

Perhaps the most enduring examples of love came from Korean coworkers, teachers, nurses, health aides, and administrators, who formed unshakable bonds with volunteers. These relationships often began formally but slowly warmed. One Korean teacher told me, "At first, I was afraid she would judge me. Then I saw her stay late to help students. I saw her cry when a child failed a test. That is when she became my friend."

There was a volunteer who worked at a local health center. The community had been skeptical of yet another foreigner, but he was sensitive to this and didn't rush to implement programs. Instead, he helped plant potatoes. He learned everyone's names. And one winter, when an elderly patient passed away, he attended the funeral and stood silently with the family. The village chief later said, "Now he is one of us."

A past volunteer was reunited with her former midwife colleague in Gyeongsangbuk-do, Mrs. Song. The two had worked side-by-side in a rural maternal health clinic from 1974 to 1976. "She used to watch me," Mrs. Song recalled, laughing, "to make sure I boiled the water long enough. I didn't mind. I knew she meant well." What began with cautious observation turned into a deep partnership. They delivered babies together, walked to neighboring villages together, and shared snacks on long, cold clinic days. Nearly forty years later, when they met at the reunion hall, Mrs. Song greeted her with tears. "I thought I might never see her again," she said, "but I kept her letters all these years."

In Gangwon-do, a former teacher, Mr. Park, and his Peace Corps partner shared their story. In 1970, they were assigned to co-teach English, an unusual arrangement at the time. "He showed up in a suit too big for him, with a bag of books and no idea what *jjigae* (a spicy Korean stew) was," Mr. Park recalled with a smile. But the volunteer had a gift for patience. He sat quietly through teacher meetings, practiced greetings in Korean every morning, and gradually earned the trust of his more senior colleagues. "At first," Mr. Park continued, "I thought, 'He is here for two years and then gone.' But he stayed in touch. Every year. He even wrote to my daughter when she was sick in college. That is not a coworker. That is family."

Another volunteer returned to Jeollabuk-do for the first time in decades and met up with her former school nurse, Mrs. Lim. They had worked together during polio vaccination campaigns in the early 1970s. "We were both young," Mrs. Lim remembered, "and the work was hard. Some days we walked for hours to reach remote children. But the volunteer never once complained." After her volunteer left Korea, they exchanged postcards and photographs. And when Mrs. Lim's son studied in the US, it was her American volunteer who met him at the airport and helped him settle in. At the Revisit, the two women embraced and spent the day walking through their old clinic site. "We were brave together," our Peace Corps volunteer said softly. "And I learned from her what it means to serve quietly, with love."

One of the most moving accounts came from a former volunteer who served in South Jeolla. She had worked closely with a Korean health aide, Mr. Choi, in a tuberculosis outreach program. He was her guide, her translator, and eventually, her closest friend. "We walked together into villages where no one wanted us," she recalled. "He told me when to speak and when to be silent." Mr. Choi, now in his eighties, spoke slowly when they were reunited: "I did not think she would remember me. But she brought a photo of us from 1975. I keep that photo now by my bedside."

These stories reveal a simple but powerful truth: when people work together in service, without ego, without hurry, they discover something deeper than cooperation. They discover kinship. The friendships formed between them were not transactional—they were transformative. They endured across borders, languages, and decades.

Love, Always often meant entering these relationships without assumptions, without fanfare. It meant letting others lead, recognizing local wisdom, and showing up day after day in the mundane and the meaningful. In doing so, our people and their Korean counterparts became more than colleagues—they became family.

And when they met again in quiet villages, there was no need to catch up on titles or accomplishments. The first words, always, came from the heart: "Do you remember…?" and was followed by laughter, tears, and the quiet affirmation that the love they built together had never disappeared.

Love During the Final Days

As the Peace Corps program in Korea neared its end, the love shared over the years became even more visible. Staff members spent extra hours helping the volunteers find jobs or graduate programs. Farewell ceremonies were organized in every region, and not because it was required, but because they wanted to express their gratitude to the people who had made them feel at home.

One such gathering in Busan stands out in my memory. A young boy presented a volunteer with a handmade paper crane. "Because you smiled at my mother when she was sick, I smile now." No policy, no budget line, no strategic plan could account for that kind of behavior and leadership. It was pure, it was quiet, and it was transformative.

This kind of love—gentle, steadfast, and human—defined the final months. It was present in the office when our Korean staff began preparing closure documents. They did not just file paperwork, they wrote handwritten notes to volunteers, translated farewell letters from village leaders, and kept detailed files in case someone might return one day and ask, "What happened to my students?"

Mr. Lee, our logistics officer, began compiling a small binder of favorite volunteer memories: photos from training, scribbled thank-you notes, holiday cards. "I want the new people who may return to this office someday, to know who was here," he said. This wasn't an official duty. It was an act of devotion and friendship.

In Jeollanam-do, a regional health officer hosted a meal for the departing volunteers. When asked why she went to such lengths, she replied simply, "They loved our people. Now we show our love to them." Over bowls of *doenjang jjigae* and freshly picked *perilla* leaves, stories were exchanged. One volunteer shared how her counterpart had walked six miles in the snow to deliver a set of student essays she had left behind. Her voice cracked as she said, "She didn't want me to think the students didn't care."

At a gathering in Andong, a Korean teacher sang a folk song, one she hummed while preparing tea with her Peace Corps co-teacher in the early 1970s. "We never said goodbye properly," she said through tears. "So I sing this now." Her former co-teacher, sat beside her, holding her hand.

Love, Always

Love was also evident in the way volunteers chose to say farewell. In Gyeonggi-do, several second-year volunteers pooled their stipends to commission a local artisan to create woodblock prints of the countryside for their schools and clinics. "We wanted to leave something behind," one said, "but something that was made here, by Korean hands." That gesture, honoring not just the work but the land and people that had embraced them, spoke volumes about the depth of connection they felt.

In the final weeks before closure, one staff member, Ms. Yoon, asked if she could spend a few days visiting the more remote sites, not to inspect but to say goodbye. "I helped train them," she explained. "I need to see how they lived, to thank the families who cooked for them and worried for them." She returned from each visit carrying small gifts—herbs, knitted scarves, handwritten notes. None of it was requested. All of it was created and given with love.

And in Seoul, during our final all-staff meeting, one of our Korean colleagues stood and bowed to the group. "We are not saying goodbye," he said. "We are bowing in thanks for teaching us, for trusting us, for walking with us." There were few dry eyes in the room.

The Peace Corps didn't leave Korea with fanfare or ceremony, but with heartfelt hugs, letters of gratitude, and promises to return. Volunteers helped their coworkers write résumés, translated applications to overseas programs, and reached out to NGOs to see if positions were open. One volunteer stayed an extra month at his own expense so he could help his school apply for a sister-school program in California. "This isn't a job," he told me. "It's a bond. Bonds don't end on schedules."

Love, Always as a leadership practice is about more than sentiment. It is about sustained attention to the well-being of others. It is about honoring the dignity of relationships, especially at the moment of parting. It is about saying with every action, "You mattered to me. You still do."

And long after the Peace Corps left Korea, that message continued to echo through letters, reunions, and in quiet moments when a former student hears an English phrase and remembers, "My teacher taught me that." Or when a health worker unwraps an old photograph and smiles at the memory of walking through rice fields with her American partner.

When leadership is rooted in love—real, persistent, humble love—it does not disappear. It lives on, quietly, in the hearts it touched.

Love After Service

Love did not end with the closing of the program. Many former volunteers stayed in touch with their Korean colleagues and families. They exchanged letters, sent holiday gifts, and in some cases, returned for reunions. I received countless updates: a former student graduating from university, a host family member recovering from illness, a colleague becoming a grandparent.

One former volunteer shared with me that her Korean co-teacher called her after twenty-five years to say, "I still keep your photo on my desk." Love is enduring. It transcends language and time.

But more than the sentiment, what moved me most was how this love continued to take the form of *service*. Not the formal, structured service of programs from years ago, but the informal, deeply personal service of lives permanently linked.

There was a volunteer who had taught English in Jeju. Years later, when he learned that his host brother had opened a small English academy, he began sending him used books from his school district in Oregon. Each box came with a letter and photos of the students who had once read those books, as if to say, "We are still learning together." When he finally returned to Korea, his host brother presented him with one of the original books, dog-eared and taped at the spine. "This is our bridge," he said. "Because of this, my daughter will go to university in Canada."

Love, Always means keeping that bridge open, even when no one is asking you to cross it.

A host mother, Mrs. Shin, told me at a luncheon in Gwangju that she still cooked *doenjang jjigae* (a hearty Korean stew with fermented soybean paste, pork, tofu, and vegetables) "just the way she liked it," though the volunteer had not visited in over two decades. "She said mine was better than the school's cafeteria," Mrs. Shin laughed, "and I believed her." Then she paused, her expression softening. "When someone remembers your food, they remember you care."

That, too, is leadership through love: the honoring of memory, the decision to continue caring long after the world has moved on.

Some of our volunteers began scholarship funds in the name of their former students. These were never announced, just mentioned in a note to the principal. "Choose one student each year who shows kindness." The principal did. Every year.

And when the volunteer who began this practice passed away, the school held a small ceremony with flowers and the inscription: He taught us kindness, and he never stopped.

Still others carried the lessons of love into their own families. A former volunteer told me she taught her children the Korean values of *jeong* and *nunchi*—affection and attentiveness to others—because "...those were the best parts of me, and I learned them in Korea."

And for our Korean counterparts, the relationships endured just as strongly. A former English teacher showed a group of us a drawer in his home labeled *Peace Corps Memories*. Inside were letters, faded photographs, and a small ceramic cup "his volunteer" had given him in 1977. "We didn't always understand each other," he said, "but we trusted each other. That was enough."

Love, Always is a leadership skill not easily measured. It doesn't live in quarterly reports or organizational charts. It lives in the quiet continuities, the birthday email sent across oceans, the photo slipped into a frame decades ago, the lesson remembered by a student who never spoke in class but still hears her teacher's voice.

It is a commitment to relationship without expiration. It is a decision to keep seeing the other, long after the world has looked away.

In every corner of Korea where a volunteer once served, and in every American community where a volunteer returned a changed person, that love still circulates quietly and unmistakably. It was and is the kind of leadership that is never finished, never withdrawn, and always, always present.

It's important to keep in mind that loving deeply is not sentimentality. Instead, it is a lived strategy...and the deepest form of stewardship. When leaders care about the people they serve, not only vis-à-vis their output or productivity but with their full humanity, they unlock loyalty, creativity, and trust.

The public servant who remembers the names of the children of the clerk, the department head who takes the time to check on a grieving colleague, the country manager who asks the office cleaner how her weekend was—these are acts of leadership as important as any policy speech or program launch...perhaps even more important.

In government, we often focus on compliance, oversight, and execution, and these are necessary. But the public servants who inspire lasting change are those who make space for kindness, for humility, for the time it takes to know people's names. I worked with a government agency director who kept a jar of blank thank-you notes on his desk. Every week, he wrote one by hand to a staff member, a counterpart, a vendor. "It keeps me grounded," he said. "And it reminds them they matter." That small practice transformed the culture of his entire team.

In international organizations where missions are complex and cultures intersect, the ability to *Lead Lightly* and *Love, Always* is indispensable. Peace Corps Korea embodied that truth. Its success rested not only on its programs, but on the relationships it cultivated. I think of the volunteer and the nurse who co-designed a health class; the student and the teacher who stayed in touch for forty years. There was a country director who asked the custodian what he thought before making a policy change. These were not exceptional moments; they were standard practice.

In private enterprises that endure, one finds this same ethic. Companies known for longevity and adaptability often share the quiet hallmark of leadership grounded in caring. Not performative *corporate wellness*, but an authentic culture of respect, listening, and mutual dignity. These workplaces attract talent, retain it, and grow it, not because they offer perks, but because they offer purpose and belonging.

The legacy of Peace Corps Korea is not only one of aid or instruction. It is a legacy of *Love, Always*—persistent, patient, and powerful. It is a model of leadership that asks not "What can I fix?" but "Who can I care for?"

To *Lead Lightly* and *Love, Always* is not idealism. It is wisdom earned through long roads and silent rooms. It is knowing when to hold back and when to reach out. It is a way of seeing people not as roles to be managed…but as lives to be honored.

This chapter, this reflection, is not just about the past. It is a call to lead wherever we are with that same spirit. With unyielding care. With steady compassion.

With *Love, Always.*

Ready to explore practical exercises and journal prompts for "Love, Always"? See the **Leadership Practice Guide** *in the back matter.*

A Korean Voice

Mrs. Bae
Former MCH Clinic Patient, South Jeolla Province
(1970s)

I was nineteen when I became pregnant with my first child. My husband worked in the fields, and I lived with his mother in a one-room house at the edge of the village. There was no hospital, only a small health clinic run by two Korean nurses, and one foreign woman.

At first, I avoided her. I was shy, and she didn't speak much Korean. But one afternoon, I fainted from dizziness while waiting for my check-up. I woke up in the clinic bed, and the American volunteer was sitting beside me, holding my hand. She had stayed through her lunch hour, watching over me as if I were her own sister. After that day, I visited the clinic more often. She would ask how I was sleeping, if I had enough to eat, if my baby was kicking. She showed me how to prepare barley water and told me softly, 'Your body is doing something strong.' When I gave birth, she came to my home the next day, bringing cloth diapers she had sewn herself. My mother-in-law was moved to tears. Not because of the gift, but because of the gesture. In our culture, that's how love is shown. Years later, when I had my third child, she was already gone. But I remembered her voice, her touch, her kindness. She wasn't just a helper. She left behind something warm, something that stayed.

LEADERSHIP TAKEAWAYS

Love, Always

Love may seem intangible in business, but it manifests as genuine care and respect for people. In the context of leadership, whether in development work, corporate settings, or community service, love is what transforms technical expertise into lasting impact.

- **See people, not roles.** Know your team's humanity. Go beyond job descriptions and titles to understand the people: their dreams, challenges, and contributions. We remember how we were treated far longer than we recall metrics or deadlines.

- **Commit without conditions.** Support others because you believe in them, not only because you're hoping for results. True commitment means offering guidance, patience, and presence, even when progress is slow or mistakes are made. It's not about waiting for people to earn your support, but about giving it because you believe in their potential.

- **Create lasting impact.** Relationships built on care outlive contracts and projects. The quiet presence of a leader who listens, encourages, and shows up fosters trust and loyalty that endure far beyond the span of a project or the walls of an office. A culture of care is not only good for morale, it strengthens teams, builds resilience, and creates legacies that extend through generations.

BOTTOM LINE: Love is leadership's greatest strength. It is the force that humanizes strategy, connects people across differences, and leaves a mark not through authority, but through presence and care. In the end, those we lead will remember how we made them feel—respected, valued, and supported. That is the true measure of leadership.

III
LEGACY

Chapter 7

SO OTHERS REMEMBER

Leadership is often taught as a path to visibility. A chance to be known, to influence, to leave a mark. But the most enduring leaders I have known, and the most lasting legacies I have witnessed, came not from those who stood at the front, but from those who chose, again and again, to walk beside.

The previous chapters are not descriptions of philosophies. Instead, they are important memories. Of a country, a people, a program, and a season of service that taught me what leadership truly means in any setting.

To lead, *Walk Slowly* is to remember that transformation takes time. In Peace Corps Korea, nothing happened overnight. Relationships unfolded slowly—one quiet walk to school, one shared cup of barley tea, one whispered word in English. Learning how walking slowly is not falling behind…it is choosing to stay present.

To lead, *Listen Deeply* is the glue. It was how we knew what people needed, even when they didn't say it. It was how a volunteer realized the co-teacher wasn't distant, just shy. How a health worker understood that what a mother needed wasn't advice, but to be heard. Listening is not just a skill. It is the sacred act of making someone feel real in your presence.

To *Lead Lightly* is not to withhold strength, but to carry it with care. In Korea, I learned that silence can speak, and gentleness can guide. I saw how pausing to ask rather than to answer opened more doors than any directive. The volunteers who sat quietly with grieving families, the staff who knew when not to speak—these were the moments when leadership was at its most powerful.

To *Lead Wisely* is perhaps the hardest. It means letting go of control. It means believing in the capacity of others, in the wisdom of a local teacher, the resilience of a volunteer, the grace of a moment I did not orchestrate. Trust is not given lightly, but once earned, it becomes the foundation on which everything else stands.

To lead with *Fierce Hope* is necessary. Looking back, I think of those days when the path was not clear, when policies changed, and when closures loomed. These were moments when grief sat too heavy in the room. But in those moments, it was hope that called us forward. Not a naïve hope, but something grounded, a quiet conviction that what we did mattered. That kindness changes things. That presence is power.

To lead with *Love, Always* is not idealism. It is a daily choice to act with care. I watched Korean coworkers stay late to translate lessons and host families knit blankets for Americans they barely knew. I saw volunteers show up for funerals, for birthdays, for the quiet everyday events that make up a life. That expression of love was not soft. It was strong. And it endured.

These are not six separate lessons. Rather, they are six ways of seeing the important elements of leadership. Six ways of serving. Six ways of remembering that leadership is not about legacy, but relationships. And when we lead this way—walking slowly, listening deeply, leading lightly, with trust, with fierce hope, and with love, always—what we leave behind is not our name. What we leave behind is a deep sense of belonging.

Years after the last Peace Corps volunteer left Korea, many memories remained. They are in drawers filled with letters, and bowls of *jjigae* still cooked "the way she liked it." There are memories we carry about the quiet pride of a former student who became a teacher…because someone once believed in him. They led because they had come to believe in themselves—as worthy, as capable, as people whose lives and voices mattered.

That is the highest purpose of leadership: not to be remembered, but to help others remember who they are.

You must lead so others remember.

Lead so when your presence is gone, the legacy of your care still lingers.

Lead so that one day, decades from now, someone in a village or a classroom or a kitchen or a boardroom says, "Because of that person, I knew that I mattered."

That is what Peace Corps Korea taught me.

And it is how I will choose to lead…always.

Chapter 8

SOME FINAL THOUGHTS

As I look back on a life shaped by service, leadership, and the quiet grace of walking beside others, I am struck by how often the most enduring lessons came, not from grand successes, but from humble and human encounters. Leadership is not a destination, but a way of being. It is less about rising to the top…and more about submerging oneself into the daily realities of others. That means walking beside them, learning from them, and growing with them.

When I first arrived in Korea in late 1978, I thought I had prepared myself. I had studied the country's history, its culture, and its politics. I believed I knew the importance of the Peace Corps' mission. I carried credentials, titles, and carefully crafted ideas and ideals. What I did not carry was a deep understanding of the people I had come to serve alongside, nor did I grasp the quiet wisdom of humility.

That wisdom came slowly. It came in the warmth of barley tea shared in drafty offices with Korean staff who had spent their careers building the level of trust I had not yet earned. It came in the silence of late-night walks through Seoul's alleys, where the weight of doubt pressed more heavily upon me than my coat. It came in the patient laughter of a senior staff member showing me how to eat a proper *ssam*, and in the quiet pain of her childhood story—one of war and resilience. These moments dismantled the scaffolding of certainty I had arrived with, and replaced it with something sturdier. That *something* was empathy.

Empathy is the soil in which trust takes root. And trust is the foundation of all meaningful leadership. The kind of trust that grows from presence. From showing up without pretense. From honoring the expertise of others, especially when it doesn't come wrapped in credentials.

Throughout my career, whether in Central Asia, the Pacific, Africa, or Eastern Europe, I witnessed how real leadership unfolds; not through grand strategies but through consistent human connections. The most effective leaders I encountered were never the loudest in the room. They were the ones who paused to understand, who paid attention to context, and who recognized the quiet strength in those seated around them.

In Peace Corps Korea, I saw the transformation that came when we took time to understand the rhythm of a place. Volunteers who leaned into this kind of presence didn't just teach or treat, they connected. They were able to see the story beneath the surface, to work not just *in* communities, but *with* them.

I also saw the power of paying attention. Not just listening to words, but listening with the whole self. The tone of a voice, the glance exchanged across a room, the silence held in a conversation. These, too, guided me to understand what needed to be said. And just as importantly, what did not.

Leadership was about anchoring myself in the wisdom of others. In Korea, our local staff, many with stories far more complex than mine, held the keys to context, continuity, and credibility. Their experience shaped decisions in ways no external manual ever could. I learned to pause, to ask, and to follow their lead.

And I witnessed courage in unexpected forms. A volunteer creating a game to teach English in a drafty classroom. A nurse running a health workshop in a room with no heat. A Korean mother standing up in a meeting to advocate for her child's right to be educated. These weren't stories of grand vision—they were stories of persistent belief that something better was possible.

Now, years later, I reflect not just on the work, but on what allowed the work to endure. The answer, I believe, is love. Love for the people. Love for the possibility that service brings. Love for a future we may never see, but one we are still responsible for shaping. This love was not sentimental. It was resilient. It showed up in the details, in the way we returned phone calls, listened without judgment, and stayed when it was easier to leave.

So, what do I know now, after a lifetime of leading, of learning, of walking beside?

> I know that presence matters more than performance.
>
> I know that humility creates space for real growth.
>
> I know that building trust requires time, attention, and honesty.
>
> I know that leadership is less about the leader and more about what others believe is possible in their presence.

And most of all, I know that to walk beside someone, to share their burdens, their hopes, and their laughter, their long silences is one of the greatest privileges of leadership.

As I close this chapter, I offer these thoughts not as conclusions, but as invitations. To future leaders, to Peace Corps volunteers still serving around the world, to anyone who seeks to make a difference:

>   Lead not with certainty, but with curiosity.
>
>   Lead not to be followed, but to accompany.
>
>   Lead not for recognition, but for relationships.

And always remember that the long arc of leadership does not bend toward glory, it bends toward connection. Toward service. Toward the quiet, steady work of building a better world, one act of trust, one act of love, one shared step at a time.

ACKNOWLEDGMENTS

In the years after my time in Korea, I returned often to the lessons I learned there—lessons not just for leadership, but for life. When challenges felt insurmountable, I remembered the jagged peaks around Seoul, the quiet resilience of volunteers, and the deep strength of our Korean partners.

Korea taught me that leadership is not about charging forward, but about presence and patience. That progress depends not on control, but on trust. And that humility, far from weakness, is what allows true change to take root.

The seeds planted by Peace Corps Korea—an English class, a health campaign, a conversation over tea—may have seemed small at the time. But they nourished something lasting. The transformation belongs to the Korean people. Still, I like to think Peace Corps helped enrich the soil.

Even decades later, I carry Korea with me—in memory, mindset, and heart.

Walk slowly. Listen deeply. Lead lightly. Trust wisely. Hope fiercely. Love, always.

Above all, I am filled with gratitude.

To the Peace Corps volunteers of Korea: Your courage and compassion shaped lives and communities. Many reflections here are drawn from your words; memories remembered with care.

To the Korean staff of Peace Corps Korea: You were the

backbone of the program. Your wisdom, patience, and example showed me what leadership looks like.

To colleagues across the globe: Your example deepened my understanding of leadership in all its cultural and human complexity.

To Friends of Korea: Your work sustains a legacy and builds bridges across generations. I invite readers to support that effort at ***www.friendsofkorea.net***.

To Jon Dunbar, for his generous support in amplifying the voices of Peace Corps Korea volunteers through *The Korea Times*, and for his insightful guidance during the early drafts of this book.

And to Victoria Zackheim, whose expert eye and steady hand brought clarity, rhythm, and refinement to these pages. Her patient, line-by-line guidance shaped the voice and flow of this book in ways I could never have achieved alone. Any remaining errors or omissions are entirely my own.

To Yongbok, my wife: You are the quiet anchor of my life.

And to all who believe that leadership is rooted in service and that even the smallest acts of presence can ripple outward: Thank you. May these stories affirm that the arc of leadership bends toward connection, humility, and love.

With enduring gratitude,

Jim

IV
FINAL TOOLS

REFLECTIONS FOR FUTURE LEADERS
Why Reflect on Leadership Now?

In a world grappling with pandemics, inequities, social unrest, and rapid technological shifts, the need for authentic leadership has never been greater. The command-and-control model struggles in today's interconnected, adaptive systems. What endures instead are quieter truths: empathy, presence, connection, and resilience.

The lessons in *The Long Arc of Leadership*, drawn from Peace Corps Korea, are not nostalgic—they are enduring. They offer timeless guidance for leaders across sectors, from rural classrooms to boardrooms, from policy desks to field teams.

1. Walk Slowly in a Fast World

Lasting leadership impact doesn't come from speed. It grows from patience, cultural understanding, and relationship-building.

Contemporary Example: Executive coach Melissa Fanaro observes, "Slowing down allows more stakeholders to contribute—generating more inclusive and innovative outcomes."

Takeaway: *Fast wins fade. Sustainable success grows through presence and trust.*

2. Listening as a Leadership Superpower

Deep listening—beyond courtesy—creates safety, builds trust, and unlocks real insight.

Contemporary Examples: Jacinda Ardern credited her COVID-19 success to listening deeply to both scientists and citizens.

Takeaway: *Listening is not passive; it transforms fear into clarity, and clarity into action.*

3. Lead Lightly to Empower Others

Leadership isn't about control; it's about creating space for others to grow.

Modern Insight: Bill Gates and Jeff Bezos gained trust by working *with* teams, not lording over them.

Takeaway: *Hold space, not reins. Empowerment outlasts oversight.*

4. Trust—The Invisible Currency

Trust accelerates collaboration and builds resilience in times of change.

Research: *Harvard Business Review* found employees at high-trust companies report:

- 74% less stress
- 106% more energy
- 50% higher productivity
- 76% greater engagement

Takeaway: *Trust may be invisible, but it powers everything that's visible.*

5. Hope—The Courage to Continue

Hope is not wishful thinking; it's resolve in the face of setbacks.

Insight: *Psychology Today* emphasizes that hope, when grounded in values, improves workplace productivity and team endurance.

Takeaway: *Hope is a discipline, not a mood. It steadies teams when the future is unclear.*

6. Love—Leadership's Quiet Core

Love in leadership means care in action—mentoring, showing up, and honoring people as more than roles.

Research: Dr. Terri Egan, professor of organizational behavior and leadership at Pepperdine University, notes, "Smart leaders legitimize and leverage emotions…to be more effective and lead more fulfilling lives."

Takeaway: *Love is not weakness. It's the strength that remains when strategy and ego fall away.*

7. Courage and Adaptability

Strong leaders stay learners—open, curious, and ready to pivot.

Modern Wisdom: Satya Nadella of Microsoft reminds us, "Don't be a know-it-all. Be a learn-it-all."

Takeaway: *Adaptability is essential. Courage means acting before you're certain.*

8. Presence Over Performance

Leadership isn't about always shining; it's about showing up when things are hard.

Reminder: Scott Monty, former head of social media at Ford Motor Company, put it well: "Anyone can steer the ship when the sea is calm."

Takeaway: *Your calm, steady presence in crisis speaks louder than charisma ever could.*

9. Humility—The Ground of Growth

Humble leadership invites trust, dialogue, and shared growth.

Perspective: Rajeev Suri, former CEO of Nokia, said, "Humble leadership earns respect without seeking attention...every interaction is a chance for mutual development."

Takeaway: *The best leaders don't claim to know everything. That's why others trust them.*

QUICK GUIDE FOR LEADERS

- **Start with presence** – Be where you are. Listen deeply.
- **Build trust through consistency** – Keep your word. Own your mistakes.
- **Empower others** – Step back so others can lead.
- **Model hope** – Frame setbacks as beginnings toward growth.
- **Lead with love** – Value people beyond roles.
- **Stay curious and adaptable** – Learn before acting.
- **Reflect often** – Leadership growth happens in moments of quiet insight.

What matters isn't your name in the history books, it's who you helped believe in themselves.

When leaders walk slowly, listen deeply, lead lightly, trust wisely, hope fiercely, and love, always—they forge a legacy of belonging, not just achievement.

The long arc of leadership bends toward connection, responsibility, and shared humanity.

THE LONG ARC OF LEADERSHIP FRAMEWORK

A Summary of Six Enduring Leadership Traits and Their Practice

TRAIT	CORE PRINCIPLE	HOW IT LOOKS IN PRACTICE
Walk Slowly	Presence matters more than performance	Show up consistently. Learn the landscape. Let others set the pace.
Listen Deeply	Understanding precedes action	Pause before responding. Hear what isn't said. Stay curious.
Lead Lightly	Influence grows when ego shrinks	Share credit. Invite collaboration. Trust others to lead.
Trust Wisely	Trust is built by giving it—carefully	Extend trust with integrity. Repair it when broken. Be transparent in doubt.
Hope Fiercely	Hope is a discipline, not a wish	Act in small, faithful ways. Hold space for uncertainty. Believe in future good.
Love, Always	Love is leadership's greatest power	Be present. Be kind. Remember. Let relationships outlast roles.

THE LONG ARC OF LEADERSHIP
Leadership Practice Guide
Discussion & Reflection Prompts

How to Use This Guide

The Leadership Practice Guide is designed to deepen your engagement with the ideas and stories in *The Long Arc of Leadership*. Whether you are reading on your own, in a leadership cohort, a classroom, or a book circle, these prompts provide space to pause, reflect, and connect the lessons to your own life and work.

Each of the six traits—Walk Slowly, Listen Deeply, Lead Lightly, Trust Wisely, Hope Fiercely, and Love, Always—offers a way of being that is less about authority and more about presence. These are not quick-fix techniques but long-arc practices that evolve over time. The questions in this guide are not meant to be rushed. They invite you to slow down, listen inwardly, and reflect on your own leadership through the lens of service, humility, and human connection.

Some questions may resonate immediately; others may challenge you or awaken forgotten memories. There is no single right way to use this guide. You might journal your responses, bring a prompt to a team meeting, or use it to open a conversation with someone you trust. The spacious layout is intentional—giving you room to write, underline, highlight, or return weeks later with new insight.

Leadership is not static, and neither is reflection. Return to this guide often. Let it evolve with you. Use it not just to lead more effectively, but more meaningfully, more humanely, and with deeper purpose in the communities you serve.

Tip: Return to your Leadership Practice Guide often. These traits aren't checkboxes, they're lifelong commitments. Feel free to request a printable PDF of the Guide at:

TheLongArcBook@gmail.com

WALK SLOWLY

- What does "presence over performance" mean in your daily interactions?
- When have you experienced the power of simply showing up?
- How do you resist the pressure to rush or multitask?
- What helps you slow down and stay grounded?
- When have you seen transformation through steady, patient presence?
- How do you prepare yourself to enter a conversation or space with intention?
- What internal habits keep you moving too fast?
- Who models the kind of calm, grounded leadership you admire?
- What would it mean to give others more space to set the pace?
- Where in your leadership are you being called to walk more slowly?

[Notes:]

_____
_____
_____
_____
_____
_____

LISTEN DEEPLY

- When was the last time someone listened to you without interrupting?
- How do you respond when you disagree; do you listen more or less?
- What habits make it hard for you to listen fully?
- What body language communicates that you are truly listening?
- How does deep listening build trust?
- Who in your life is a model of compassionate listening?
- What happens when you pause before responding?
- What assumptions often block your ability to listen?
- How might you listen to those who feel invisible?
- How can you practice listening beyond words—tone, silence, and feeling?

[Notes:]

_____
_____
_____
_____
_____
_____
_____
_____

LEAD LIGHTLY

- What's the difference between leading and controlling?
- Where do you feel the need to be the expert, and what happens if you're not?
- How does leading lightly show respect for others' contributions?
- Who on your team might rise if you stepped back?
- What would it look like to delegate more generously?
- How can light leadership still be strong leadership?
- What fears keep you from leading lightly?
- How does your ego influence your leadership?
- What are the quiet signals that you're holding on too tightly?
- How do you share success and celebrate others?

[Notes:]

_____
_____
_____
_____
_____
_____
_____
_____
_____
_____

TRUST WISELY

- What criteria do you use to decide whether to trust someone?
- What is your earliest memory of trust being built or broken?
- How can you rebuild trust once it's been damaged?
- Where do you hesitate to trust, and why?
- How can leaders create safe environments that encourage trust?
- What's the cost of withholding trust too long?
- What systems do you have in place to maintain transparency?
- Who in your leadership life models trustworthy behavior?
- What is the difference between trusting someone and agreeing with them?
- Where is trust being tested in your life right now?

[Notes:]

_____
_____
_____
_____
_____
_____
_____

HOPE FIERCELY

- What's one story of hope that has stayed with you?
- How do you hold onto hope in uncertain times?
- What's the difference between hope and optimism?
- What would fierce hope look like in your community?
- Where do you see signs of quiet, resilient hope?
- What role does hope play in long-term leadership?
- How does hope relate to action?
- How can you help others recover hope when they feel defeated?
- Who gave you hope at a pivotal time in your life?
- How do you stay hopeful while still facing hard truths?

[Notes:]

LOVE, ALWAYS

- How do you define love in a leadership context?
- What does it mean to lead with kindness in tough situations?
- How do you care for those who are hard to love?
- What does "let relationships outlast roles" mean to you?
- Who modeled love as a leadership trait in your life?
- What simple actions can embody love in your work?
- When have you seen love transform a broken situation?
- What does it look like to lead with both heart and boundaries?
- How do you express care across differences?
- How can love be your guide even when no one's watching?

[Notes:]

_____
_____
_____
_____
_____
_____
_____
_____
_____
_____
_____

BIBLIOGRAPHY

Appadurai, Arjun. 2004. "The Capacity to Aspire: Culture and the Terms of Recognition." In *Culture and Public Action*, edited by Vijayendra Rao and Michael Walton, 59–84. Stanford, CA: Stanford University Press.

Bellah, Robert N., Richard Madsen, William M. Sullivan, Ann Swidler, and Steven M. Tipton. 1985. *Habits of the Heart: Individualism and Commitment in American Life*. Berkeley: University of California Press.

Bennett, Milton J., ed. 1998. *Basic Concepts of Intercultural Communication: Selected Readings*. Yarmouth, ME: Intercultural Press.

Block, Peter. 1993. Stewardship: Choosing Service Over Self-Interest. San Francisco: Berrett-Koehler.

Brown, Brené. 2018. *Dare to Lead: Brave Work. Tough Conversations. Whole Hearts*. New York: Random House.

Clifford, Mark L. 1998. *Troubled Tiger: Businessmen, Bureaucrats, and Generals in South Korea*. Armonk, NY: M.E. Sharpe.

Cumings, Bruce. 2005. *Korea's Place in the Sun: A Modern History*. Updated edition. New York: W. W. Norton & Company.

Cvetkovich, George, and Timothy C. Earle. 1995. *Social Trust: Toward a Cosmopolitan Society*. Westport, CT: Praeger.

Freire, Paulo. 1970. *Pedagogy of the Oppressed.* New York: Herder and Herder.

Gambetta, Diego, ed. 1988. *Trust: Making and Breaking Cooperative Relations.* Oxford: Blackwell.

Heifetz, Ronald A., and Marty Linsky. 2002. *Leadership on the Line: Staying Alive Through the Dangers of Leading.* Boston: Harvard Business Review Press.

Hoffman, Elizabeth Cobbs. 1998. *All You Need Is Love: The Peace Corps and the Spirit of the 1960s.* Cambridge, MA: Harvard University Press.

hooks, bell. 2000. All About Love: New Visions. New York: William Morrow.

Kelley, Nancy. 2016. "Revisiting Korea: Reflections of a Peace Corps Volunteer." *Peace Corps Korea Revisit Program: A Celebration of Shared History, 2008–2016,* 55–58. Seoul: Korea Foundation.

Kilburn, Benjamin. 2020. "Listening and Learning: Cross-Cultural Peacebuilding in Korea, 1966–1981." *Journal of Peace Corps Studies* 2 (1): 45–64.

Korea Foundation. 2016. *Peace Corps Korea Revisit Program: A Celebration of Shared History, 2008–2016.* Seoul: Korea Foundation.

Martin, William. 2004. "Hope as a Framework for Educational Development in Post-War Societies." *Comparative Education Review* 48 (4): 423–438.

Mishler, William, and Richard Rose. 1997. "Trust, Distrust and Skepticism: Popular Evaluations of Civil and Political Institutions in Post-Communist Societies." *Journal of Politics* 59 (2): 418–451.

Noddings, Nel. 1984. *Caring: A Relational Approach to Ethics and Moral Education*. Berkeley: University of California Press.

Palmer, Parker J. 1998. *The Courage to Teach: Exploring the Inner Landscape of a Teacher's Life*. San Francisco: Jossey-Bass.

Park, Young-sook. 2009. *A History of Education in Modern Korea*. Seoul: Yonsei University Press.

Schein, Edgar H. 2013. *Humble Inquiry: The Gentle Art of Asking Instead of Telling*. San Francisco: Berrett-Koehler.

Ting-Toomey, Stella. 1999. *Communicating Across Cultures*. New York: Guilford Press.

Vorhis, Linda. 2016. "Small Triumphs." *Peace Corps Korea Revisit Program: A Celebration of Shared History, 2008–2016*, 91–93. Seoul: Korea Foundation.

Weick, Karl E., and Kathleen M. Sutcliffe. 2007. *Managing the Unexpected: Resilient Performance in an Age of Uncertainty*. 2nd ed. San Francisco: Jossey-Bass.

Yarrow, Andrew L. 2010. *Measuring America: How Economic Growth Came to Define American Greatness in the Late 20th Century*. Amherst: University of Massachusetts Press.

INDEX

A

adaptation, flexibility 30, 36, 43–44, 69–71, 75, 155
Ardern, Jacinda 154
assertiveness 37, 40, 46

B

Bartlett, Sarah 13
belief. *See* leadership, enduring truths
belonging
  efforts in 69–71, 75, 79–80, 121
  feeling valued 15, 27, 57, 111, 121
Bezos, Jeff 154
birth attendants/midwives 21, 23, 79. *See also* healthcare

C

Carter, Tom 38
Cho, Helen 39
Choi Mi-kyung 107
Christopher, John 17
Civitan International 3
Cold War 37, 68
compassion. *See also* leadership, enduring truths
  for children, mothers 24, 26–29
  for the ill 13, 15, 62–63, 78, 113
  leading, listening with 5, 30, 45
Conant, Doug 98
confidence, courage 18, 20, 59, 111, 155
Confucianism 17, 36
Connelly, Julia 23
Cornbluth, Sue 103
Crosby, Anne 28
curiosity
  creating space for 18
  framing challenges 115
  leading with 148, 155
  observing to understand 32, 36, 37–38, 39, 42–43, 51, 71

D

Douglass, Dan 103

E

education
  Korean classrooms
    group-oriented 44
    hierarchy of 17, 81, 104
    Korean teachers 19, 31, 39, 45, 51, 75–81, 95–96
    strict curriculum 38, 47, 95
  Korean teachers 48, 122, 125
  scholarship funds 131
  student confidence, courage 18, 20, 59, 111
  Western, informal methods 8, 17–20, 45, 104
Egan, Terri 155
empathy 11, 35, 47, 55, 75, 146
empowerment 53, 65, 98
encouragement 18, 77, 107, 109, 115, 137

F

Fanaro, Melissa 153
Fine, Elizabeth 104
Fritts, Marsha 110

G

Gates, Bill 154
Gorman, Mary Beth 37
Grandis, Donald 105, 106

H

Hahm, Bob 103
Harvard Business Review 154
healthcare
  co-workers, volunteers 62, 77, 113–114, 125
  leprosy 13, 15, 62–63, 78
  maternal, child health 8, 21–28, 105, 121, 135
  polio vaccination campaign 126
  tuberculosis 113, 126
Hess, Don 71
humility 18, 30, 40, 71, 80, 97, 146, 156
Hwang, Peter 15

J

Jon Keeton 4

K

Kelly, Nancy 105
Kim, David 13, 104
Kim Jeong-sook 107
Knudsen, Robert 109
Korea
  Friends of Korea 29
  Gwangju Uprising 84–86
  healthcare shifts 80
  Host Country Request Model 72–75
  industrial boom 44
  Korea Foundation Revisit Program 79
  Korean War 3, 36
  Ministry of Education, Health 23, 72, 89
  NGOs on disability rights 27
  Park Chung-hee (President) 36, 83
  Peace Corps program closes 29
  political upheaval 83–85
  post-War 36, 38, 56, 67, 72
  rural conditions 36
  United States partnership 55
Korean people/culture

Confucianism 17, 36
cultural exchanges 18, 38
determined, resilient 2, 7, 21, 69, 146
disabled children 3, 25
food, drink
  bulgogi 5
  doenjang jjigae 5, 37, 123, 125, 128, 131, 143
  hotteok 5
  makgeolli 37, 70
  namul 123
  perilla leaves 128
foreigners and 39, 56, 57, 68, 72–75, 135
gender, hierarchy 17, 43, 81, 104
healthcare workers 62, 110, 125
hospitable, compassionate 5, 69, 102, 110, 120, 123–124, 127–128
host families 12, 39, 41, 44, 68, 123–124, 131
Korean Peace Corps staff
  become family 5–7, 125–132
  collaboration 48, 92
  identity 104
  supportive, supporting 4, 5–7, 88, 106–108, 110, 120
language/terms
  bogeonso (health center) 105
  Chuseok (holiday) 56
  hanbok quilt 123
  hyung (older brother) 56
  If you go slowly, you go far 31
  janggi (Korean chess) 14
  jeong (affection) 132
  learning Korean 20, 103–104
  nakkyeoja (leper) 13
  nunchi (attentiveness) 132
  sanhujori halmeoni (postpartum grandmothers) 21
  seonsaengnim (teacher) 75, 81, 86
  yangnomo (foreigner) 75
silence 39, 52, 89, 126

understanding 32, 36, 37–38, 39, 42–43, 51, 71
See also education
Krzic, Gerry 29

L

Ladd, Margaret 22
leadership, enduring truths
  conceptions of 35, 55, 67, 101, 119, 141
  principles in practice 159
  hope fiercely
    a discipline, not mood 116, 155, 159
    believing in others 104–105
    curiosity 18, 39, 115, 148, 155
    facing unknown 101–102, 103, 117, 142
    Peace Corps legacy 105–109, 109–112
    reflections 155, 171
    resilience, courage 114, 115, 155
  lead lightly
    empathy 55
    empowerment 65, 154
    humility 142, 159
    reflections 154, 167
    strength 64, 142
  listen deeply
    actively/between the lines 37, 51, 88, 146, 154, 159
    as cultural exchange 38, 47
    compassion 5, 6–7, 30, 44, 45, 46, 59
    core skill, discipline 41, 49–53
    empathy, humility 35, 40, 45, 47
    reflections 154, 165
    respect, trust 24, 31, 37, 51, 52, 141
    silence 46, 62, 125
    to suffering 5, 6–7, 44, 45, 46, 59, 113
  love, always
    daily choice 122, 132, 142
    leadership's greatest strength 138, 155, 159
    manifested 27, 119–122, 137
    reflections 155, 173
  trust wisely
    bridging differences 67–71, 77, 81, 88–90, 132
    daily practice, long-term 86–88, 92–94
    empathy, humility 71, 75, 80, 97, 146, 156
    empowering others 97, 98, 142, 154, 155, 159
    establishing 4, 14, 22, 47, 72–81, 97, 121
    fragility of trust 90–92
    presence 75, 97
    reflections 154, 169
    solidarity 7, 29
  walk slowly
    building trust 11, 24, 32, 153
    empathy, humility 11, 18, 30, 40
    patience 7
    presence over performance 29, 32, 141, 156, 159
    reflections 153, 163
Lee, Marcia 18
Lee, Michael 39
leprosy. *See* healthcare

M

McAllister, Jeannie 14
Meyers, Katherine 26
Monty, Scott 156

N

Nadella, Satya 155

O

O'Donnell, Kevin 30, 64
O'Donnell, Michael 19
O'Neill, Timothy 25

P

Park Chung-hee (President) 36, 83
Park Seung-ho 107
patience 7, 47, 78, 97, 110, 121
Peace Corps Korea
  community services, training 12, 71
  Country Directors 1, 4, 57, 67, 71, 133
  50th anniversary reunion 49
  Korean staff
    become family 5–7, 125–132
    collaboration 48, 92
    identity 104
    supportive, supporting 4, 5–7, 88, 106–108, 110, 120
  legacy of 48, 87, 133
  program ends 29, 57–61, 128–129
  reciprocal listening, trust 48, 93
  shifts healthcare 80
  volunteers requested 11, 47, 72, 73
Peace Corps volunteers
  alter perception of foreigners 20, 39, 56, 57, 68
  become part of village/family 24, 69–70, 86–88, 103, 121, 123–124
  begin scholarship funds 131
  compassion, bridging differences 15, 23, 24, 47, 121–122, 131
  emotional toll on 15, 24, 102, 110
  inspire students 59–60, 76, 102, 104, 111, 121, 131
  learning Korean 20, 103
  "led with their ears" 19
  observing to understand 32, 36, 37–38, 39, 42–43, 51, 71
  political unrest and 83
  returnees/revisits 79, 86–88, 105, 107–108, 123–125
  shared mission 81–82, 116
  skills, task alignment 26, 35, 74
  training 21
  walking/standing beside 23, 59
performance 29, 32, 141, 156, 159
polio vaccination campaign 126
prenatal care 23. *See also* healthcare
presence
  building trust 11, 75, 97, 146
  compassion 27, 36, 45, 136
  over performance 29, 32, 141, 156, 159
  silence 46, 62, 125
Psychology Today 155

R

relationships
  local wisdom 21–28
  long-lasting 16, 20, 29, 56–57, 79–80, 86–88, 130
  prioritizing 32, 47
resilience 69, 114, 115, 154. *See also* leadership, enduring truths
respect
  elders, authority figures 37, 42, 81, 90
  listening 37, 40, 47
  local customs, wisdom 21–28, 32, 41–43, 47, 133

S

silence 46, 62, 125
solidarity 7, 57
Special Olympics 3
Stephens, Kathleen 12
Suri, Rajeev 156

T

Taylor, Alan 104
tuberculosis 113, 126. *See also* healthcare

V

Vasquez, Anna 19

Y

Yi Kyung-pyo 106

ABOUT THE AUTHOR

James E. H. Mayer has spent over five decades in public service—spanning continents and crises—walking the long arc of leadership with purpose, humility, and resolve. He has held leadership positions within the Peace Corps and USAID across Asia, Africa, the Pacific, and Eastern Europe, working with diverse communities and complex development and diplomatic challenges.

As the final Peace Corps country director for Korea, Mayer oversaw one of the agency's most culturally impactful programs, shaping enduring ties between the United States and the Republic of Korea. He later served as country director in number of Peace Corps countries, and held leadership roles in USAID missions in Africa, Central Asia, Eastern Europe, and the Pacific. In every assignment—from rural African field teams to crisis response efforts in the Pacific—he exhibited a leadership style grounded in patience, listening, and respectful collaboration.

Mayer is a graduate of Pepperdine University. He has received numerous awards including the Civilian Honor Award from the Republic of Korea, the Golden Heart Award from the Philippines, the Paul Harris Fellow Award from Rotary International, and the USAID Innovation Award. His legacy includes mentoring dozens of emerging leaders, directing some of the largest Peace Corps operations worldwide, and advancing reforms that improved program delivery and staff development.

He serves on the boards of Friends of Korea and the LAX Kiwanis International Foundation, and is a trustee of the Orange County World Affairs Council in Irvine, California.

Mayer is the author of two previous books: *Winding Through the Clouds* and *The Resting Place: Thoughts Along the Way*, both personal collections of reflections spanning a life of service.

He is married to Yongbok Lee Mayer and resides in Mission Viejo, California. Together, they are blessed with a large and vibrant family that includes twenty-three grandchildren and eight great-grandchildren (at the time of this printing).